A WINTER IN MAJORCA
(1838-1839)

GEORGE SAND

A WINTER IN MAJORCA
(1838-1839)

FOREWORD BY
LUIS RIPOLL

Translated by Lieut. Colonel W. Kirkbride

1970

Original Title:

UN HIVER À MAJORQUE

Dep. legal: P. M. 1649-1970

PRINTED IN SPAIN
IMPRESO EN ESPAÑA

___

Imprenta Mossèn Alcover — Calatrava, 68 — Palma de Mallorca (España)

George Sand, by Augustus Charpentier (a work which gives one an idea of the outstanding and attractive personality of the authoress).

Frederick Chopin. A pencil drawing for the double portrait of Chopin - George Sand, by Delacroix.

PREFACE

A FEW BACKGROUND WORDS

I think it is interesting and almost obligatory, out of consideration for the reader, to include in the explicit pages of the present book, words in the original French of «Un Hiver à Majorque», which we could describe as words of circumambience and clarification. This we can justify by the very nature of the work, by its descriptive rather than its narrative character, by the superficiality and even the arrangement of some of the chapters, as well as by its subjectivity which leads the authoress at times to make cutting, doubtful or false asseverations, and to divulge ideas which with the passing of time have merited a different and even contrary qualification. In my opinion, this additional touch will, I think, be well received by the reader who makes contact, perhaps for the first time, with the romantic writer; and especially if, besides, he becomes acquainted with Majorca through these same pages, or wishes to compare his own impressions of the island with those of Aurora Dupin, alias Madame Dudevant, and George Sand in her literary works.

On the other hand an attempt has also been made to avoid an excessive number of notes, combining my own with the already numerous notes of the authoress and the translator.

The first thing you should be told is that the winter to which the book refers is the famous one of 1838-1839. In reality it was not a winter, but part of the autumn and a little more than half of the following season. A particular note should be made of this point, because the authoress herself, in the work we are prefacing, is mistaken; she is under the impression that she was in the island a month longer then she actually was.

We know of course all about those remote days which witnessed the visit of this early tourist from the 11th November 1838 to the 13th February 1839. We must say at once that George Sand did not make the journey alone. She was accompanied by Frederick Chopin, the immortal musician, her children, Maurice and Solange Dudevant, as well as by a French maid. The latter is presented to us as a shadowy figure, but nevertheless she played a quite important role during the travellers' Majorcan days.

The scene of their stay was first, Palma (which, contrary to what the authoress states, was formerly called Ciutat de Mallorques until the 17th century), then a house in a suburb of the capital called Establiments, and finally, from the 15th December until their departure, the Carthusian monastery (Cartuja) of Jesus the Nazarene in Valldemosa. The monks had abandoned this monastery, not of their own desire, but following a governmental law called the «Ley Mendizábal»; which must have been of a tremendously advanced nature for those days, and which was designed to take away or, at least, reduce the power and multiple riches that the ordinary religious Orders had succeeded unlawfully in retaining. Under this law, which was put into force at different periods, the dissolution of the Order was brought about and either the demolition of their convent, or only its secularization. An example, among several others, of the first case is the demolition of the convent of Santo Domingo, situated close to the Cathedral of Majorca, a Gothic gem, whose blessed and moving ruins the writer of this book was still able to gaze upon. And an example of the second case is the Cartuja of Valldemosa and its monks.

8

The Mendizábal law opened the way for George Sand and more than her, her companion, to make this building famous throughout the world; because the result was that, once the religious inhabitants had gone, the Government decided to divide the monastery up, and to dispose of or let the cells and some of the outbuildings to private individuals. At first the Majorcans had some objections to taking possession, whether by purchase or transfer, of property which for them continued to be of the Church. But they soon forgot these scruples, apart from the fact that the Church covered them by its ordinances, after payment of the corresponding benefactions which absolved them from the sinful responsibility arising from the wrongful acquisition of certain possessions.

In one of the secularized cells of the Cartuja of Jesus the Nazarene, in which some political refugees had lived, or maybe in two, George Sand installed herself with her family on the 15th December 1838.

Throughout the story we shall hear mention made of revolution and revolutionaries, of refugees from unpopular decrees. What was happening in those days in Spain? What was happening in the traditionally tranquil island of Majorca? The Spanish people were still in the throes of the civil war, a war caused by a dynastic dispute: on the one hand Bourbons (supporters of Isabel II, then on the throne and of a democratic tendency), and Carlists on the other. George Sand tells how explosions could be heard at night near the powerful walls of Barcelona, and how she could still see the traces left by the recent passage of troops in the outskirts of the Catalan capital. In Majorca, which was in the hands of the Government, there was not much enthusiasm for new ideas, which were opposed by the barrier of their spotless religious sentiments; or better to say, by their intransigence in the matter of the Catholic religion; not, in truth, in a profound Christian sense. Carlism, it can be said, was relegated to the aristocratic class alone.

Anyway, the Majorcans felt the violent effects of the revolution. And only a week before the visitors set foot ashore,

9

the «Diario Constitucional de Palma» had published, by way
of a supplement to its issue of the 5th November, a decree
declaring a state of war in the whole district of Majorca, all
the inhabitants becoming subject to military law. This was
something very serious.

George Sand, who makes so many illogical and laborious
digressions in the book which you, the reader, have in your
hands, attributes the reason for this state of emergency that
was still in force when the travellers boarded the ship for
their return home, to causes which are only figments of her
imagination. If she had had the good fortune to know about
this decree (published so few days before her arrival), as I
now have since it is on my table as I write, she would have
seen that it was purely precautionary.

There had appeared in the island armed parties who committed robberies and other crimes, and it was feared that
there would be infiltrations by the opposite faction. «The
enemies of the Constitution and of the throne of Queen Isabel II wish to cause in this loyal province» the decree pro-
claimed, «the same evils that unhappily are being experienced in other provinces of the peninsula». And further on it
was added that the crimes which would be tried by the military courts would be «espionage, disclosing information,
complicity or co-operation with the enemy, sheltering the
enemy, conspiracy, any machination or act in aid of the
enemy calculated to disturb the public peace, the spreading
of news liable to discourage the troops or the people...
etc., etc.».

With this sword of Damocles over the island's head, and
with the National Militia placed under the command of Lieu-
tenant-General of the Regular Army and Captain-General of
the Balearic Islands, Don Pedro Villacampa Maza de Lizana,
it surprises me that George Sand didn't encounter yet more
difficulties than she actually did. Moreover, the mistrust of
the country people, which she talks so much about, is justified, at least in a general sense, by these same military measures. In Majorca there is a maxim that advises one, when
there is a war on, to speak in a low voice, «Parlau baix per

10

que estam en guerra» (speak low, there's a war on), and it was precisely in a state very like war that the authoress found us Majorcans in 1838.

The reserve of the islanders, both city and country dwellers alike, was therefore perfectly justified, and George Sand records it as follows: «The prudence of the Spaniard and the distrust of the islander reach such limits that a foreigner must not ask anybody a question of the very slightest importance, unless he or she wishes to run the risk of being taken for a political agent». Naturally, this statement does not preclude that the Majorcan countryman is suspicious by nature. Then and now.

The book most widely read about this island, the one we are lightly commenting on, is divided into three parts, as the reader will be able to see immediately for himself. These parts correspond to other equally long articles or instalments published in each of the editions of the «Revue des Deux Mondes». The first four chapters of Part I are devoted to describing the island, with extracts taken from here and there. In the geographical and geopolitical part, as we would say now, George Sand makes use of the «Description of the Pityusian and Balearic Islands, Madrid, 1787», which was brought to her attention through an account written by another French person, the diplomat Andres Grasset de Saint-Sauveur, who knew the island at the beginning of the 19th century and published an interesting book.

In regard to her descriptions of monuments or objects of artistic appeal, she either reproduces Tastu, or has recourse to the «Souvenirs d'un Voyage d'Art à l'Île de Majorque», which was published with interesting illustrations in 1840 by Joseph Bonaventure Laurens, a French antiquarian in matters of art. The latter author sent his book to the authoress in Paris, which had the effect of reviving her Majorcan memories; for by then time had somewhat dimmed her recollections of the whole episode with Chopin and her children, and the maid called Amélie, about whom we now know something more.

The story of the visit really begins in chapter V with

*their arrival in Palma in the month of November 1838, on
the 8th instant at half past eleven in the morning, on the
brandnew and (for those days) excellent steamer, called «El
Mallorquín», whose details and seaworthiness we know all
about, but which in consideration of the brevity of this preface I will pass by.[1]*

*Chapters V, VI, and VII concern their settling in, the
difficulties they encountered, and the move to «Son Vent»,
which has been freely translated as «House of the Wind».
«Son» is a possessive which is frequently met with in Majorca, and means «This belongs to...» or «Property of...».
«Son Vent» should really be defined as the wind's domain,
or windy, or perhaps by some cognomen as «Vent» (Wind),
despite the fact that this property in the district of Establiments is not in a particular stormy area. Son Vent is in a
surpassing locality inland, on fairly high undulating ground
in the proximity of Palma, and very near to the bed of a
watercourse called «Sa Riera», which is dry for most of the
year, and crosses the city to flow into the harbour close to
the ramparts.*

*This stretch of the Majorcan countryside gives occasion
to George Sand to make an inspired eulogy of the island's
scenery, as she does later on about Valldemosa. She only
knew the island very partially; nevertheless its physical features captivated her. For example she says:*

*«For painters, Majorca is one of the most beautiful places
on earth, and one of the least known.» «Majorca is the Eldorado of painting. Picturesque beauty is everywhere.» «Everything seems to be presented with a kind of euphoria for
the delight of the eye.» «It is green Helvetia under a Calabrian sky, with the solemnity and silence of the East.» These
remarks, chosen from many more, serve as excellent and valuable advertising slogans today.*

1.   A detailed account of this journey is to be found in my book
The Majorcan Episode of Chopin and George Sand, where many details about the voyage can be found, as well as information about this
steamship, known throughout the Palma docks as "Es Pagès" (the
countryman). (Edition in English.)

Chopin at the piano. George Sand is listening to him. This work by Delacroix doesn't exist as a complete picture, as it was cut in half by an unknown hand. Today their portraits are kept separate.

tual á las tres
D. José Est
entresuelo.

Press cutting, announcing the departure of the «El Mallorquin», in which George Sand and Frederick Chopin travelled to Palma and back, from Barcelona.

It is common knowledge that everything that George Sand puts on the scales in praise of Majorcan nature and scenery, is counterbalanced by detractions and opinions that are anything but complimentary for the Majorcans of those far-off days. I am not going to make a study of each one of George Sand's views about the people, their customs, their food, and the treatment accorded her, or rather, the general indifference with which she was received.

These opinions were refuted at that time with an equal passion by a young Minorcan, who later became one of Majorca's most notable historians, José María Quadrado. Actually he regretted the words he used when he reached an age of discretion. His refutation was entitled «A Jorge Sand. Vindicación» (To George Sand. Revenge). It appeared in a small publication called «La Palma», a literary review of quite good quality but of reduced circulation, in March 1841, just after the appearance of «L'Hiver».

Quadrado reminds us a little of one of those rather unpolished Majorcans who made an unclimbable wall of their religion, glorying in patriarchal customs and in a morality which was, to the eyes at any rate, spotless. Anything that bordered on the sexual outside the strict limits of matrimony was considered a grave sin. In the first place, he saw that the author of «Lelia» was not alone; that she had with her a man who was not her husband, children of another man, and that she was dressed in clothes that outraged his rigid sense of propriety. And so, right at the start, he says that she was in «doubtful company», Chopin's, and calls her «an adventuress and a street-walker».

Quadrado, a young man in his early twenties, was a spectator of this episode. We know that she received a cold welcome, and was expecting something different. Some people had read «Lelia», and I fear me that more than one Majorcan would have liked to change places with Chopin; but this was never mentioned outside the confines of the men's clubs, of which several had just been opened. It seems to me that the well known incident of the Marquis of La Bastida's coach which everybody quotes who has spoken about this

13

affair, including Quadrado in his «Revenge», must have been an incident in which the nobleman walked very warily, not wishing to compromise himself in the eyes of island society. The Marquis of La Bastida was a young «lion», who assuredly would have enjoyed associating with the authoress more but for the «tongue-waggers» and the social conventions to which the Majorcan people have always been so attached. He offered her his carriage, and also his elegant company. Quadrado unintentionally denounces him by saying that Madame Dudevant «was indebted to this gentleman for a thousand courtesies and attentions». The young «lion», however, must have thought one day that he was going too far and began to hedge. George Sand reacted as any woman would have done, feeling slighted and angry. And so she rejected the carriage which on a certain occasion had to go up to Valldemosa, conveying not the Marquis as had been arranged, but «his respectable uncle» (quoted also by Quadrado) on a visit to his property there. Sand found other more amusing company.

Returning to the authoress's viewpoints, it is necessary to say, on the other hand, that no one can claim to being misled if controvertible and private opinions are expressed in this book. Bear in mind that she was looking at everything through coloured glasses. The intimacy of George Sand and Chopin, which she wished to turn into a new experience, taking her to an unknown and mysterious landscape and setting, full of perils, was undoubtedly a failure. Among other things, because a sick man, whose illness was aggravated there, felt in need not of intimate relationships but of care and attention; and these could not be provided in the measure and form that his lady companion wanted. Without any doubt, Sand was more his nurse than his mistress. «Our invalid», «one of us», are expressions which she constantly uses in this book we are about to commence, when referring to the composer of the «Preludes». Her state of mind shows through perforce. It is not I who say that, but she herself when she affirms «I never felt in a settled frame of mind in that country (Majorca)», or when elsewhere she adds «If I

14

write about them, I shall do so with bitterness». It is of course pure prejudice.

Perhaps an understanding, on the part of the Majorcans, of how best to treat her, or even an appreciation then of her literature, could have created better considered relationships; although anyone will doubt it who can read between the lines in that famous «Revenge», whose closing words are these:

«George Sand is the most immoral of writers, and Madame Dudevant the uncleanest of women»; words which we would not apply today to a cheap prostitute.

In the second part of her work George Sand, falling back sometimes on Laurens and other times on Grasset de Saint-Sauveur, describes Palma, the houses of the nobility and the principal monuments. Palma's typical patios with their tidy architecture did not appeal to the authoress. The ostentatious show of menials and old servants who swarmed through the palaces in such numbers that even today they are called «the family», is brought to George Sand's notice; the sight of that army of present and former domestics gave her the impression «more of halting places for caravans than of proper houses».

She visits the Cathedral which hardly draws her attention, and which she describes as gloomy where everything is brightness, even with the majority of the large windows walled up, as they were in those days. She doesn't notice or is purposely silent about the effects of the light, as it filters through the small eye-holes opened provisionally in the stone blocks of the ogival openings, and falls in oblique rays on the walls and flooring at the luminous hours of midday and afternoon. The Cathedral of Majorca, resplendent and with the choir still in the centre, can be everything but gloomy. The only thing she fixed her regard on was the tomb of Jaime II, ordered to be erected by Carlos III, placed before a passageway between the choir and the chancel, like an immense soup tureen, and perhaps the least artistic object in the Holy Church. George Sand had doubtful tastes.

In this second part she pays a visit to the ruins of Santo

15

Domingo, which she calls the Convent of the Inquisition, although that tribunal never assembled there. Her error arises perhaps from the fact that many leading Dominicans were inquisitors, and that lists of penitents were posted up in the central courtyard of the said monastery.

The literary fruit of George Sand's trip to Majorca was her novel «Spiridion», written for the most part and finished off in Valldemosa, «to the howling of the north wind in the ruined cloisters». In her descriptions there is a mixture of the Cartuja and Santo Domingo, the former being well preserved with its church almost intact, and the latters having been demolished a few years before her arrival. Some descriptions which figure in the novel of which the novice Spiridion is the chief character, could very well form part of the material in «Winter in Majorca», and conversely, chapter IV of the second part of the latter is exactly like an instalment taken from «Spiridion»; in other words, an extract from one of her works put into another.

The last part of «Winter in Majorca» is entirely devoted to Valldemosa; and in it the genius and figure of her companion seem to acquire more grandeur. She writes about his illness, the doctor who attended him (I have it confirmed that not one but three doctors attended him in Majorca), and about his tuberculosis; and about the crisis Chopin underwent in the cell, of which she gives a graphic description. Here also her attitude towards the Majorcans again comes out. She speaks of her children and their good health. «We now had enough on our hands with a sick person» she writes; and adds some words which sound rather like the key to all her ill-humour: «But the other one, far from getting better, got steadily worse what with the damp atmosphere and the privations. Despite being badly reported on by the doctors in Palma, he was not suffering from any chronic complaint; but the lack of a nutritive diet had left him, after an attack of catarrh, in such a state of languor that he couldn't overcome it». The reader will already know, however little he may have read about the life of Frederick Chopin, that there were signs of consumption from his childhood onwards. But

16

it was here, and thanks to those Majorcan doctors (whose names we even know and how much they charged for their visits[2]), where for the first time the disease was diagnosed.

«*George Sand, writes Gabriel Alomar, in his magnificent preface to the first edition in Spanish of "Un Hiver à Majorque", like Balzac, worked at night. And from the pages of Spiridion we can mentally reconstruct her restless vigils in the Cartuja, when she felt herself surrounded by the graves of the monks, and close to the cloister where superstition, which is a form of poetry, recreated the ghosts of the dead, wandering Carthusians, in whose hollow orbits was carried a vision of the unknown and the earthly truth. Perhaps there remained in the corners of the defiled cells an echo of divine colloquy or a residuum of heavenly glory.*»[3]

George Sand takes pride in being an observer, and incorporates with a sure touch in different Majorcan scenes features not in any way or but little distorted, and certain points of complete authenticity. For example, when she says that meat is leathery, she is making a statement that is still correct today, as when she brands the Majorcan olive oil as being bad. Actually, until very few years ago, this oil of very high acidity used to give off an unmistaNable odour in the country, when people were frying with it. When she speaks about the roads, she is absolutely right. Seen from the air, Majorca looks like a kind of spider's web, whose threads are the roads. By this very fact that there are so many, it has not been possible to look after them properly, and this still applies today. All the travellers of a hundred years ago or more described them as impassable.

In regard to the problems which George Sand had with the shopkeepers, and the latters' apparent rapacity, perhaps the fault may lie with that almost anonymous attendant who acted as George Sand's maid. It is very possible that she was

---

2. See Luis Ripoll, *The Majorcan Episode of Chopin and George Sand*. (Edition in English.)

3. George Sand, *A Winter in Majorca*. Translated and annotated by Pedro Estelrich, with a preface by Gabriel Alomar. Palma 1906.

17

2

the author of the pilfering and shortages that are immediately attributed to the people in Valldemosa. George Sand herself in a letter to her friend Madame Marliani almost confirms this for us. This does not mean either that these people, who were very poor, faced with the possibility of some small business, would not exploit it beyond reason. It has always happened that way with us Majorcans, who don't have Moorish, Phoenician, if not Jewish blood in our veins for nothing.

In the book there is an obvious exaggeration which I wish to draw attention to; I am referring to the allusions to the weather, to the bad weather. Here in the island, definite periods of wet and dry have never been fixed. It rains heavily or it rains lightly, and what is remarkable is that one never knows when spells of good or bad weather, of dull skies or sunshine, of rainfall or drought, are going to happen in the various seasons of the year. For example, you can enjoy a fine October and November in Majorca (as occurred with our visitors), and you can have a bad December and January, or it can be the other way round. According to George Sand January was unbearable, and yet there are years in which the «Calmas de enero» (January Calms) and the blossom on the almond trees make those days the most delightful of the year. The climate of the equinox and of the Majorcan winter is utterly unpredictable and changeable.

However, rendering honour afresh to George Sand, we have to say that the Majorcan people have not even attempted, except in our present days (and then only in the towns) to avoid the cold with rational measures. Comfort in Majorca didn't exist in 1839, not even in the lordly mansions, despite the opinion of the aforementioned Majorcan historian, José María Quadrado. There was nothing colder than those big rooms in «ses cases de senyor», the palaces of the nobility, so difficult to heat on account of their great size. The Majorcans have made too much use of an idea, which has become a standpoint: «It is never cold here». At the time of George Sand is was so, and nobody tried to do any-

18

thing about it. It was another cause for the failure of her visit.[4]

Finally, the contradictory nature of this book was undoubtedly assisted by Chopin's often mentioned illness; that, and his need of the piano which he had bought from Pleyel in Paris, choosing it himself and ordering it to be sent out to Majorca. Deluded Chopin! Visionary George Sand! Majorca in those days of 1838 was (and still is in certain aspects of transport, in spite of thousands of aeroplanes landing and taking off) a «Finisterre», one of the last corners of the world. It could take a year to send something there from Paris.

There is no more to say. I hope these comments may make the perusal of «A Winter in Majorca» easier and more pleasant for the reader; and exceptionally so for all who know the island, or who are interested by some angle of the French authoress's work, and in the musician who, on Majorcan soil and particularly in Valldemosa, composed some of his matchless pages of music.

LUIS RIPOLL

---

4.   Even nowadays it is terribly cold in winter in many Majorcan country, village and town houses. They don't mind being right in a cold draught, for they live with the doors open or not properly shut. Generally speaking, the country people have not yet learnt what really comfort and warmth mean.

LETTER FROM A FORMER TRAVELLER
TO A STAY-AT-HOME FRIEND

SEDENTARY as you are by force of circumstances, my dear François, you must think that I, carried away by the unruly and fickle hobbyhorse of my independent will and nature, have known no greater pleasure in this world than that of crossing seas, mountains, lakes and valleys. Alas! In spite of everything, I have to confess that my most beautiful and enchanting journeys have been performed by the fireside, with my feet on the warm hearth, and my elbows resting on the threadbare arms of my grandmother's arm-chair. Doubtless you will have done the same, just as pleasant as mine, and a thousand times more poetical. That is why I counsel you not to regret too much having missed sweating under a tropical sun, having your feet frozen on snow-covered polar wastes, frightful, storms lashing the sea, attacks by bandits and other dangers, or any of the hardships which you face every night in your imagination, without taking off your slippers, and with perhaps the only annoyance of some slight cigar-burns on the folds of your dressing-gown.

In order to reconcile you to having been deprived of the wide open spaces and a life of physical activity, I am sending you an account of the last visit I made outside France, in the certainty that I shall arouse your compassion rather than your envy, and that you will consider that I have paid too high a price for some outbursts of admiration and a few hard-won but ill-fated hours of delight.

This story, written a year ago, has brought upon me one of the most fulminating and laughable diatribes from some natives of Majorca that I think I have ever read in my life. It is a pity that it is too long to be published as an appendix to my story, for the tone in which it is conceived and the grace of the reproaches addressed to me, would confirm my affirmations on the hospitality and the delicacy with which the Majorcans welcome strangers. It would be a justificatory document and quite interesting, although who would venture to read it right through? Besides, if it is considered vain and stupid to disclose the compliments that one receives, would it not be even more inane and foolish, in these modern times, to make a fuss about the slander of which one is the object?

I won't then bother you with it, limiting myself to tell you, in order to complete the necessary details about the ingenuous Majorcan people, that after having read my narrative, the cleverest lawyers in Palma to the number of forty, so I've been told, met together to concoct among them a really dreadful indictment against the "immoral writer", who had taken the liberty of making fun of their love of pecuniary gain and their painstaking dedication to the breeding of pigs. As the "other one" has said, they certainly had between them all a very great inventive faculty.

But let us leave these good people in peace, who were so enraged against me. Since then they have had time to calm down, and I also have had time to forget the way they behaved with me and mine. Among the inhabitants of that beautiful island I can remember now only five or six persons whose cordial welcome and kindly attitude will always last in my memory as a recompense and one of fate's good turns. I will not name them, as I don't consider myself to be such an important person that I would be honouring them with my gratitude. But I am sure — and I think I have stressed this in my story — that they will have retained a friendly

22

memory of me, which will prevent them believing themselves included in my irreverent jibes, and doubting my feelings for them.

I have said nothing to you about Barcelona where, however, we spent some quite busy days before embarking for Majorca. To go by sea from Port-Vendres, with the weather fine and in a good steamer, is certainly a delightful trip. We began by meeting again off the coast of Catalonia the springlike air which we had breathed in November in Nîmes, but which we had left behind us in Perpignan; and by contrast, a summer heat was awaiting us in Majorca. In Barcelona a fresh sea-breeze tempered the power of a brilliant sun and swept the clouds away from the widespread horizon, bounded in the distance by mountain-tops, some black and bare, others white with snow. We had a short excursion into the country when the good Andalusian horses had eaten, having planned beforehand to return in good time to the shelter of the walls of the citadel, to avoid any evil encounter in the dark.

You well know that at that time (1838) the factionists were roaming round the district in wandering bands. They were cutting the roads, invading small towns and villages, imposing tribute on the most insignificant dwellings, quartering themselves in large houses only half a league away from the city, and emerging suddenly from every rocky hiding-place to demand his money or his life from the passer-by.

We ventured nevertheless to go some leagues away from the sea, and in the whole stretch we only met some detachments of "Cristinos" (supporters of Queen Regent María Cristina against the pretender Don Carlos), on their way to Barcelona. They told us they were the best troops in Spain. Indeed they were men of fine presence and well enough equipped to go to war; but some of the soldiers were quite thin, with yellow, wan faces, whilst their horses were showing bones through their flanks; on seeing which, we sensed the evil effects of hunger.

A still more depressing sight was that offered by the fortifications raised around the most humble settlements and poorest hovels. Sometimes the defences consisted of a small circular wall of hand-packed dry stones, and an embattled tower, high and massive, before each doorway. Elsewhere there were strong walls with loopholes around the houses, which testified that no inhabitant of this rich region felt himself safe. In many places these small nests of resistance, partly in ruins, bore traces of recent attack and defence.

Once through the immense and formidable fortifications of Barcelona, consisting of I don't know how many gateways with draw-bridges, sally ports and bastions, nothing would suggest inside that the city was in arms. Behind a triple line of cannons, and isolated from the rest of Spain by brigandage and civil war, the brilliant youth of Barcelona took the sun on the Ramblas, a long avenue lined with trees and buildings, similar to our boulevards. The women, beautiful and gracious, were concerned only with the folds of their mantillas and with the subtle play of their fans. The men, busy with their cigars, laughing, chatting, ogling the ladies or talking about the Italian opera, apparently were not interested in what was happening outside the walls. But when night came, and the opera was over, the guitars silent, and the city handed over to the care of the vigilant night-watchmen, nothing was heard above the monotonous noise of the sea except the sinister shouts of the sentries, and the even more sinister detonations which, at irregular intervals, protracted or abrupt, sometimes close by other times far off, didn't cease until dawn. Then everything became silent for one or two hours, and the citizens slept deeply, whilst the port came to life and the crowds of seamen began to stir around.

If in his or her spare moments someone dared to ask what those strange and frightening noises during the night were, the smiling reply would be that they concerned nobody, and that it was wiser not to inquire further.

PART I

CHAPTER I

About fifty years ago, two English tourists discovered the valley of Chamonix, according to an inscription carved on a rock standing on the approach to the glacier, Mer de Glace.

The claim is rather a tall one, if we consider the geographical position of this valley, but it is a fair one to a certain extent if these two tourists, whose names I can't remember, were the first to bring to the attention of poets and painters those romantic places, where Byron dreamed of his wonderful and dramatic poem, Manfred.

It can be said in general that Switzerland was not discovered for the outside world and for artists before the end of the last century. Jean Jacques Rousseau is the veritable Christopher Columbus of alpine poetry, and, as Monsieur de Chateaubriand has truly observed, he is also the father of romanticism in our language.

Not being precisely worthy of the same entitlements to immortaly as Jean Jacques, but thinking of those of which I might be justifiably proud, I believe I could perhaps have distinguished myself in the same manner as the two Englishmen of the valley of Chamonix, and claim the honour of having discovered the island of Majorca. But the world has become today so exacting that it would not be enough to have my name carved on some Balearic rock; a true description would have been demanded of me, or at least a sufficiently poetical account of my excursion so that tourists, encouraged by my words, would feel tempted to undertake one too. But as I was not in an ecstatic frame of mind in that land, I renounced then the glory of my discovery, and recorded it neither on rock nor on paper.

If I had written under the influence of the worries and frustrations which I suffered at that time, it would not have been possible for me to boast about this discovery, and more than one of my readers would doubtless have told me that it could not be so bad as made out; and yet there certainly was something to write about, for Majorca is, especially for painters, one of the most beautiful places on earth, and one of the least known. There, where it is only possible to describe the picturesque beauty, literary expression is so poor and inadequate that I never dared attempt it. The brush and pencil of the artist are necessary to reveal the graces and grandeurs of nature to the visitor. And today, if I am shaking off the sloth from my memory, it is because I found on my table, a few days ago, a beautiful book with the title of *Souvenirs d'un Voyage d'Art à l'île de Majorque* ("Recollections of an artistic visit to the island of Majorca"), written by J. B. Laurens.

For me it was a real joy to rediscover Majorca, with its palms, its aloe trees, its Arab monuments, and its Grecian style of dress. I recognised all the places with their poetical colouring, and I relived all the impressions which I thought I had effaced from my mind. There was not a hut, ruin or bush, that did not awaken in me a world of memories, as one says today; and then I felt, if not the impulse to tell the story of my journey, at least the desire to review and report on that of Laurens, the intelligent and assiduous artist, to whom must be awarded the honour, which I was attributing to myself, of having discovered the island of Majorca.

That journey of Laurens's to the middle of the Mediterranean, to shores where the sea is at times as inhospitable as the inhabitants, is much more meritorious than the excursion of our two Englishmen to the Montavert. Nevertheless, if European civilization could arrive at the point of doing away with customs officers and revenue guards, those manifestations of mistrust and national antipathies, if communication by steamer could be organised direct from our country to those parts, Majorca could very soon compete with Switzerland; for people would be able to get there in very few days, and would assuredly find there equally exquisite scenery and the same sublime grandeur, which would bring fresh themes to the painter's art.

But truly, in all conscience, I can only recommend this excursion to artists, both robust in body and of ardent spirit. The day will come no doubt when those seeking rest, and even beautiful women, will be able to go to Palma with no greater fatigue and trouble than that with which they now go to Geneva.

Having been associated for a long time with the artistic works of Taylor on France's ancient monuments, Laurens decided last year on his own account to visit the Balearics, about which he had so little information that he confesses to experiencing a deep emotion on stepping ashore there, where possibly many disappointments were awaiting him in answer to his golden dreams. But what he had gone there to look for he was to find, and all his hopes were realised. Therefore, I repeat, Majorca is the Eldorado of painting. Everything is picturesque in the island, from the peasant's cottage, which has preserved traditional Arab architecture in its minor features, to the urchin in his rags, glorying in his "magnificent uncleanliness" as Henry Heine said apropos of the vegetable market in Verona. The character of the landscape, richer en vegetation than that of Africa, is more spacious, more tranquil and natural; it is like a green Helvetia under a Calabrian sky, with the solemnity and silence of the Orient.

In Switzerland the torrents which pour down everywhere, and the incessantly passing clouds, give a constantly changing colour to the panorama, and, so to speak, such a continuity of movement that the scene cannot be fitly portrayed on canvas. Nature seems to be mocking at the artist.

By contrast, in Majorca, it appears to be waiting for him and inviting him. There, the vegetation takes on strange, arrogant forms, but never displays that irregular extravagance under which very often the outlines of the Swiss landscape disappear. The mountain top delineates its well profiled contours against a brilliant sky, the palm tree tilts over some chasm without its stately foliage being disarranged by a capricious breeze, and even the minor, stunted cactus by the roadside seems to sit there and catch the eye with a sort of presumptuousness.

First of all we will give, in more or less ordinary encyclopaedic form, a brief geographical description of the major Balearic isle. This is not so easy as one might be led to think, especially when the data has to be obtained in the place itself. The prudence of the Spaniard and the distrust of the islander are carried to such an extreme that a foreigner must not ask any question of the least imaginable importance of anybody, unless he wants to run the risk of being taken for a spy. The good Laurens, for daring to make some notes in a ruined castle whose aspect drew his attention, was arrested by the suspicious governor, who accused him of drawing a plan of the fortifications.[1] And so our traveller, determined to complete his scrap-book in any place other than a State prison, took very good care not to ask anything except about the mountain foot-paths, and to consult other documents than those dealing with the stones of ruins.

1. "The only thing that drew my attention on this river-bank was a structure the colour of dark ochre, surrounded by a hedge of cactus. It was Soller castillo. I had hardly sketched a few lines when I saw advancing on me four individuals with such a terrible look on them that I was inspired with amusement rather than with fear. Apparently I was guilty of drawing a plan of a fortress, contrary to the laws of the country, and would be thrown into prison.

I didn't know enough Spanish to explain to these gentry the absurdity of their action, and I had to appeal for help to the French consul in Soller. Despite his intervention I was a prisoner for three mortal hours, guarded by Señor "Six-fingers", the governor of the fort, a veritable dragon of the Hesperides. At times I felt like hurling this comical dragon and his ridiculous uniform into the sea from the top of his tower, but his appearance disarmed my anger. If only I had had Charlet's talent, I would have passed the time studying my governor, for

After having spent four months in Majorca, neither would I have found out more than he, if I had not consulted the little information available about it. But here my doubts began again, for the various works on the subject, already out of date, contradict each other, and travellers disprove and slander one another in such an extraordinary manner, that it is necessary to rectify some inaccuracies in order to save committing many more.

Here then, despite everything, is my geographical description of the island. And so as not to depart from my rôle of traveller, I begin by declaring that it is incontestably superior to all those that have preceded it.

he was an excellent type to caricature. Besides, I forgave him his excess of zeal on behalf of State security. It was very natural that this poor fellow, not having any other distraction than smoking his cigar and gazing out to sea, should seize the opportunity I gave him of varying his occupation. I returned therefore to Soller, laughing good-humouredly at the idea of having been taken for an enemy of the Fatherland and of the Constitution." (*Souvenirs d'un Voyage d'art a l'île de Majorque,* by J. B. Laurens.) (*Author's note.*)

31

CHAPTER II

Majorca, which Laurens calls Balearis Major, as the Romans did, and which the king of Majorcan historians, doctor Juan Dameto, says was formerly known as Clumba or Columbia, in reality receives its name from a corruption of the Latin word for it. The capital has never been called Majorca, as many of our geographers are in the habit of saying, but Palma.

This island is the biggest and most fertile of the archipelago, which is the remains of a continent whose low-lying regions must have been invaded by the Mediterranean; and which, having once without doubt united Spain with Africa, shares the climate and produce of both. It is located 25 leagues (approx. 100 miles) to the south-east of Barcelona, 45 leagues (approx. 180 miles) from the nearest point on the African coast, and I think 95 to 100 (380-400 miles) from the port of Toulon. Its area is 1,234 square miles.[1] its perimeter 143, its greatest dimension 54 and its smallest 28. The population, which in the year 1787 was around 136,000, is

---

1. "Medida por el ayre. Cada milla de mil pasos geométricos y un paso de 5 pies geométricos." (Miguel de Vargas, *Descripciones de las islas de Pitiusas y Baleares*. Madrid, 1787.)

now approaching 160,000; the city of Palma has 36,000 inhabitants, as opposed to 32,000 at that time.

The temperature varies considerably in the different seasons. The summer is extremely hot on the plain, but the climatic conditions in winter are greatly influenced by the ranges of mountains which run from the north-east to the south-west; which bearing demonstrates Majorca's identity with the territories of Africa and Spain, whose nearest points take on the same relative direction, and have corresponding salient angles. Thus, Miguel de Vargas relates that in the Bay of Palma, during the terrible winter of 1784, the Réaumur thermometer registered 6 degrees below zero (− 18.5 F) one day in January, that on other days it went up to 16 (68 F), and generally remained at 11 (57 F). This temperature was approximately what we had in an ordinary winter in the mountains of Valldemosa, which enjoys the reputation of being one of the coldest places in the island. On the severest nights, when the ground outside was covered with two inches of snow, the thermometer fell to 6 or 7 degrees (45-48 F). At 8 o'clock in the morning, it rose to 9 or 10 (52-54 F), and towards midday reached 12 or 14 (59-63 F). Normally, towards three in the afternoon, the hour when the sun disappeared from view behind the mountain peaks that surrounded us, the thermometer again fell rapidly to 9 and even 8 degrees (50 F).

The north winds frequently blow there with great violence, and in some years the winter rains fall with an abundance and continuity of which we haven't the least idea in France. In general, the climate is healthy and mild in the whole of the southern region which faces towards Africa, being protected from the furious storms of the north by the mountain range and by the considerable cliffs lining the northern shore. In fact, the island is like a plane inclined from north-east to south-west; and navigation, which is almost impractible in the north on account of the jagged projections and precipices along the "rugged, horrible, shelterless, dangerous" (Miguel de Vargas) coast, is easy and safe in the south.

In spite of its hurricanes and rough spells, Majorca, which was with much justification called the Golden Isle by the ancients, is highly fertile, and its produce is of a very fine quality. They grow such a pure and beautiful wheat that the inhabitants export it, and it is used exclusively in Barcelona to make a type of white, light pastry known as *pan de Mallorca*.[2] The Majorcans themselves import a cheaper wheat of inferior quality from Galicia and Biscay, on which they live; and so it is brought about that, in a country where excellent grain is grown, the bread is horrible. I don't know if this transaction does them any good.

In our central provinces, where agriculture is very backward, the farmer's methods only proclaim his obstinacy and ignorance. The same thing with greater truth applies to Majorca, where agriculture, although very thorough and widespread, is in its infancy. Machines, even the simplest, are unknown; the men's arms, thin and weak as they are in comparison with ours, suffice for everything; but with an unheard-of slowness. Half a day's work is necessary to dig less earth than is dug in two hours in our country; five or six of the strongest men are required to move a load which the smallest of our porters would carry happily on his shoulders.

In spite of this indolence, everywhere is cultivated in Majorca and, as far as one can tell, well cultivated. Poverty, as we know it, is unknown among these islanders; yet, in the midst of nature's treasures and under the most beautiful sky, their life is harder and more dismally dull than that of our countryfolk.

Travellers are accustomed to make epigrams about the gaiety of these southern people, who appear on Sundays in their picturesque costumes smiling in the sunshine, and whose lack of ideas and foresight they take for the ideal serenity of the country life. It is a mistake that I myself have

2. I don't know any roll or cake of this name. She is confusing it, perhaps, with the "coques" (small breakfast rolls), or with the "ensaimades" (a typical puff pastry in spiral form).

The speculation to which she refers later has ceased. (*Translator's notes.*)

35

sometimes made, but I am cured of it since I've seen Majorca.

There is nothing so poor and sad in the world as this country person who only knows how to pray, sing and work, and who never thinks. His prayer is a stupid formula which he doesn't understand; his work is an operation of the muscles which he is unable to improve by any intellectual effort; and his song is the expression of a melancholy that unconsciously dejects him, and of whose moving poetry he seems to be quite unaware. If it were not for the vanity which from time to time awakens him from his torpor and incites him to dance, he would spend his fiesta days sleeping. But I am going beyond the limits I set myself. I am forgetting that, following the usual customs, a geographical article must first of all describe the commercial and productive economy, and only devote its attention to Man in the last place, after the cereals and live stock.

In all the geographical reference books I have consulted, I have found this brief description in the section on the Balearics, and I transcribe it here without prejudice to my pointing out later certain factors that moderate its accuracy:

"These islanders are very friendly. (We know that in all islands, the human race is divided into two categories: those who are cannibals, and those who are very friendly.) They are gentle, hospitable, they rarely commit crimes, and theft is almost unknown among them." Further on I will come back to this subject.

But, firstly, let us talk about production. For, from what I hear, some words (indiscreet to say the least) have been spoken in the Chamber, on the possible occupation of Majorca by the French; and I imagine that if this manuscript falls into the hands of one of our deputies, he will be more interested in what I say about the produce of the country than by my philosophical reflections on the intellectual capacity of the Majorcans.

As I have said then, the soil in Majorca is wonderfully fertile, and with a more intense and intelligent system of cultivation the output could be increased tenfold. The most important products for export consist of almonds, oranges and pigs. Oh beautiful plants of the Hesperides, guarded by those foul dragons! It is not my fault that I am forced to link your memory with that of these ignoble animals, which the Majorcan tends more jealously and proudly than your sweet-smelling flowers and your golden apples! However this Majorcan fellow who cultivates you is no more poetical than the deputy who reads my writing.

I will get back to my pigs. These animals, dear reader, are the most handsome on earth. Dr. Miguel de Vargas has, with the frankest admiration, drawn a picture of a hog which, at the early age of one year and a half, weighed twenty-four *arrobas,* that is, six hundred pounds. At that time the exploitation of the pig did not enjoy the importance that it does today. The live stock industry was obstructed by the rapacity of the contractors and purveyors to whom the Spanish goverment entrusted, or rather sold, the business of victualling. By virtue of their discretionary powers, these said speculators opposed all exportation of cattle, and reserved to themselves the right of importing it without limitation.

This usurious practice resulted in the farmers neglecting the rearing of live stock; meat fetched a very low price and, export trade being prohibited, they had no other course than to give it up completely or ruin themselves. The extinction of the herds of cattle was rapid. The historian I have quoted recalls with sadness and nostalgia the times when the Arabs ruled the island; for then, on the mountain of Arta alone, they bred more fecund cows and noble bulls than could be counted today on the whole of the plain of Majorca.

This waste was not the only thing that deprived the country of its natural riches. The same writer relates that the mountains, especially those of Torrella and Galatzo, were covered in their time with the most beautiful trees in the world. There was an olive that measured twenty-four feet in circumference and fourteen in diameter; but these magnificent woods were devastated by the shipwrights who, on the occasion of the Spanish expedition against Algiers, used their

37

timber for the construction of a complete fleet of gunboats. The annoyances to which the owners of these woods were subjected at that time, and the miserly indemnification awarded to them, induced the Majorcans to destroy their woodland resources instead of increasing them. Nowadays the vegetation however is so abundant and beautiful that it doesn't occur to the visitor to lament the past; but now as then, and in Majorca as in all Spain, corrupt practice is still the predominant factor. Nevertheless, the visitor never hears a complaint, because, when an unjust regime takes over, the weak and helpless are silent through fear, and when a wrong is done, they go on being silent through force of habit.

Although the tyranny of the monopolists has disappeared, the flocks have not recovered from their ruination, nor will they do so while the right to export remains limited to the pig industry. Very few oxen and cows are to be seen in the lowland regions, and none in the mountainous part. Generally speaking their flesh is lean and leathery. The sheep come from a beautiful pure-bred stock, but are poorly nourished and badly cared for; and the goats, which are of an African breed, don't give one tenth as much milk as ours do.

The ground lacks manure, and in spite of the eulogies the Majorcans lavish on their methods of farming it, I believe that the seaweed they use is a very poor fertilizer, deficient in humus, and that the land does not produce what it should under such a generous sky. I have carefully examined the very beautiful wheat which the inhabitants don't think worth eating; it is exactly the same as we grow in our central provinces, and which our country-people call white wheat or Spanish wheat; it is equally beautiful in our country, despite the difference in climate. The Majorcan wheat should, however, have a marked superiority over ours, which has to contend with severe winters and unreliable springs. And yet our agriculture is also very primitive, and we have much to learn in this respect; but the French farmer displays an energy and perseverance which the Majorcan would scorn as being a waste of excitement.

Figs, almonds, olives and oranges are produced in abundance in Majorca; but as there is an absence of roads in the interior of the island, trading in them lacks development and organization. At the spot where they are gathered, oranges are sold at five hundred for about three francs; but to have such a voluminous load transported on an animal's back from the centre of the island to the coast, it is necessary to pay almost as much as the cost of the merchandise itself. This consideration results in the orange industry being neglected in the interior of the country. Only in Soller, and in the neighbourhood of the coves, where our small vessels can go and load up, are these trees grown in large numbers. However, they could flourish everywhere, and in our mountain retreat of Valldemosa, one of the coldest places in the island, we had lemons and magnificent oranges, although they were rather later than those in Soller. In La Granja, situated in another mountainous region, we have picked lemons the size of one's head.[3] It seems to me that the sole island of Majorca could supply the whole of France with these exquisite fruit, at the same price as we pay for the wretched oranges we get from Hyères and the Genoan coast. This industry, so boasted about in Majorca, is then, like the rest, thwarted by a wilful neglect.

The same thing can be said about the enormous crop of olives, which are certainly the finest in the world, and which the Majorcans, thanks to Arab traditions, know how to cultivate perfectly. Unfortunately they only know how to obtain a rancid and repulsive oil from them, which would cause us a veritable nausea, and which they would never be able to export in any quantity except to the Spanish mainland, where there is an equal liking for this foul oil. But the peninsula itself is also very rich in olive trees, and if Majorca supplies it with any oil, it must be at a very low price.

In France we consume a large quantity of olive oil, and it is very unsatisfactorily marketed at an exorbitant price. If our manufacturing processes were known in Majorca, if the

3. Obvious exaggeration. Perhaps they were bitter orange or citron trees. (*Translator's note.*)

island had roads, and lastly, if merchant shipping was properly organized in that direction, we would have oil at a much lower price than we are paying; and, moreover, it would be pure and plentiful, however rigorous the winter might be. I well know that the manufacturers who cultivate the olive tree in France choose to sell a few tons of the precious liquid for their weight in gold, which our grocers then proceed to swamp in casks of peanut and rape oil, to offer it to us at "cost price". But it would be excessively obstinate on our part to persist in producing this commodity in a difficult climate, if we could procure it better and cheaper only twenty-four hours distance away.

However, our tradesmen need have no fears. Even if we promised the Majorcans and the Spanish in general to get our supplies in their country and vastly increase their wealth, they wouldn't alter their ways. They so profoundly disdain any improvements from abroad, and especially from France, that I doubt whether they would agree to change the way of life inherited from their forbears, even for money — that money which nevertheless they don't usually despise.[4]

4. This oil is so offensive that, in the island of Majorca, houses, inhabitants, conveyances, and even the air in the fields, are all impregnated with the odour. As it is used in all the cooking, in every house vapours from it arise two or three times a day, and the walls are saturated with it. Deep in the country, if you lose your way, you have only to sniff the air, and if you catch the smell of rancid oil in the breeze you can be sure that behind some rock, or hidden in a clump of cactus, you will find a habitation. If in the wildest and most deserted spot this odour still pursues you, look up and you will see a Majorcan on an ass about a hundred yards away coming down the hill towards you. This is not a joke nor a hyperbole; it is the plain unvarnished truth.

CHAPTER III

Not knowing how to fatten the cattle, nor utilize wool, nor milk the cows, for he detests milk and butter as much as the hates work — not knowing how to produce enough wheat to bother about eating it, nor grow mulberry trees for the cultivation of the silk-worm — since he has lost the art of carpentry, once flourishing in the island and now completely forgotten — seeing that he has no horses, because Spain in maternal fashion requisitions all the foals in Majorca for use in her army, for which reason the islanders don't care to appear so silly as to work just to maintain the country's cavalry — and as he does not consider it necessary to have a single highway nor a practicable track in the whole of the island, as long as the right to export is surrendered to the whim of a government that has no time to attend to such trifles — the Majorcan then was vegetating, without anything else to do other than tell his beads and mend his breeches, more worn out than Don Quixote's, his patron saint in misery and arrogance, until the pig came along to save everything. When the export of this animal was sanctioned, a new era began, the era of salvation.

In future times, the Majorcans will call this century the

age of the pig, in the same way as the Mussulmans recount in their history the age of the elephant.

Today, neither the olives nor the carob beans lie neglected on the ground, nor are the prickly pears just play things for the children. The housewives are now learning to make economical use of broad beans and potatoes. The pig doesn't permit anything to go to waste, for it eats up all it can find; it is the finest example of liberal voracity, coupled with the greatest simplicity in tastes and habits, that the world has to offer. And so, in Majorca, it enjoys rights and privileges which, up to the present, one hasn't dreamed of according to man. Dwellings have been enlarged and made airier, fruit which used to rot on the earth is now gathered, graded and preserved, and steam navigation, which previously was considered superfluous and senseless, has been established between the island and the continent.

Thanks also to the pig, I have visited the island of Majorca, for if I had thought of going there three years ago, I would have had to give up the idea of making a long and dangerous voyage in a sailing ship. But since permission was given for the exportation of the pig, civilization has penetrated the island. A small and beautiful steamer has been purchased in England, of a tonnage not big enough to compete with the terrible winds of northern regions, but which, when it is calm, transports two hundred pigs and a few passengers as extras once a week to Barcelona.

It is quite touching to see the care and tenderness with which these gentlemen (I don't mean the passengers) are treated, and with what gentleness they are deposited on land. The captain of the steamer is a very agreeable man who, by force of living with and talking to these noble beasts, has acquired a voice rather like their grunt, and at the same time a little of their impudent look. If a passenger complains of the noise they are making, the captain replies that it is the sound of gold falling on the counter. If some lady is prudish enough to complain of the foul odour permeating the whole ship, her husband is there to tell her that money never smells bad, and that without the pigs she would have

42

neither silk clothes, French hats, nor mantillas from Barcelona. If a passenger is sea-sick, it's no use his asking for help from some member of the crew, for the pigs also get sea-sick, and with them this illness is accompanied by a certain exhaustive lassitude, and a readiness to lie down and die that has to be combated at all costs. Then, forgetting all compassion and sympathy in his anxiety to preserve the lives of his cherished patients, the captain in person, armed with a whip and followed by sailors and cabin-boys, each one carrying whatever comes ready to hand — some with a crowbar, others with a belaying pin — hurls himself into the middle of the pigs; and very soon, the whole mute and recumbent herd of swine, paternally thrashed, is compelled to get up, stir about, and in this violent fashion fight off the deadly influence of the rolling ship.

When we returned from Majorca to Barcelona in the month of March,[1] the heat was stifling; yet it was not possible for us to go up on deck. Although we would have braved the danger of having our legs bitten by some ill-disposed pig, the captain would not have allowed us to upset his precious cargo with our presence. They were very quiet during the first hours of the voyage, but at midnight the first mate noticed that the animals were very dejected and drowsy, and seemed to be getting into a state of the blackest depression. Then it was that the whip was applied; and regularly every quarter of an hour we were awakened by such frightful howls and whines, produced partly by the screams of pain and rage of the flogged pigs, and partly by the shouts and oaths of the captain, swearing at and urging on his subordinates, that many times we thought the herd was devouring the crew.[2]

Once we anchored in the port, we longed to do nothing but get away from such strange society, and I confess that

1. She didn't go in March, as mentioned in the preface, but on the 8th February 1809. (*Translator's note.*)
2. Absurd statement on George Sand's part. This does not mean that pigs prone to seasickness would not grunt to the rhythm of the waves beating against the ship, which the authoress would confuse with flogging. They are, of course bad travelling companions. (*Translator's note.*)

that of the islanders too was beginning to weary me as much as the other; but we were not permitted to emerge into the open air until the pigs were landed. We could have died from asphyxiation in our cabins without anybody worrying about it while there was a pig to disembark or cure of seasickness.

I am not afraid of the sea, but one of our party was dangerously ill. The crossing, the bad smell, and the lack of sleep hadn't helped to ease his sufferings. The captain had exhibited no other sign of attention to us than to ask us not to put our invalid into the best bunk in the cabin for, according to Spanish prejudice, all illness was contagious; and as our friend had already decided to have the mattress on which the sick person was lying burnt, he wanted it to be the one most worn out. We sent him back to his pigs. A fortnight later when we went back to France on board the *Phénicien*, one of our country's magnificent steamships, we compared the delicacy of the French with the so-called hospitality of the Spanish. The captain of the *Mallorquin* had argued about a bed for a dying man; the captain from Marseilles, on seeing that our invalid was not comfortable, took the mattress from his own bed to give it to him. When I wanted to pay for our passages, the Frenchman observed to me that I was giving him too much money; the Majorcan had made me pay double.[3]

From all this I am not inferring that man is exclusively good only in one corner of this terrestrial sphere, nor exclusively bad in another. In mankind, moral evil is no more than the outcome of material misfortune. Suffering engenders fear, mistrust, fraud, and strife in all its senses. The Spaniard is ignorant and superstitious; consequently he believes in contagion, is frightened of sickness and death, and is devoid of faith and charity. He is unhappy and overbur-

3. The theories about contagion are confirmed by medical science. With regard to the payment of double the value of the fare, this assuredly is a falsehood, seeing that it would be obtained at the fixed price at the company's office. The offices of the steamer "El Mallorquin" were in the Calle de Morey in Palma. *(Translator's note.)*

dened with taxes. As a result he is grasping, egoistic, and deceitful with foreigners. In history we have seen that the Spaniard, where it has been possible for him to be great, has demonstrated that he has greatness in him; but he is a man, and in private life succumbs to all the things that man gives way to.

I found it necessary to state these preliminaries before writing about the people such as I found them in Majorca; and I hope I may be excused from talking further about olives, cows and pigs. The length itself of this part of my story is not in very good taste. I must ask forgiveness from whoever may consider themselves affronted by it, and I will now take up my tale seriously. I believe I could limit myself to following Lauren's narrative step by step; but on the other hand I think that too many thoughts will assail me when I tread once more in my memory the rugged foot-paths of Majorca.

CHAPTER IV

"But if you don't understand anything about the art of painting", people will say to me, "what the devil were you doing on board that wretched galley?"

I would like to bore the reader as little as possible talking about "me" and "mine"; however, I shall be obliged frequently to say "I" and "we" when describing what I have seen in Majorca; for such is the accepted method of expressing one's incidental thoughts and feelings, without which I could not have revealed certain aspects of the reality of Majorca, which might be useful to the reader. I therefore beg the latter to consider my personality as something quite passive, like a magnifying glass through which he will be able to see what happens in that distant country, about which one applies the proverb, "it is better to believe it than go there and see it". Furthermore I must warn the reader that I am not trying to interest him in the trifles that concern me, for I am being led by a somewhat philosophical objective in relating them here. When I have formulated my ideas in this respect, I hope that he will do me the justice of acknowledging that there is not the slightest trace of vanity in my story.

I will tell the reader outright, then, why I was on that "wretched galley"; in a few words, I wanted to travel. And

I in my turn will ask my reader a question: "Why do you travel, my dear friend, why do you do it?" Already I can hear you replying in the same words as I would use in your place: "I travel in order to travel". I well know that travelling is a pleasure in itself; but behind it all, what is it that impels one to indulge in this costly, tiring, and sometimes dangerous pleasure, which is always attended by innumerable disappointments? The need to travel. Well then, tell me: What is this need, why does it obsess us all in a greater or less degree, and why do we all give way to it, even after we have so often realised that it is an obsession with us that we can't throw off and never satisfy?

If you don't wish to answer me, I will take the liberty of doing it for you. It is that, in reality, we are never completely happy at any time in our lives, and whatever our conception may be of the ideal (or if you don't like this word, one's understanding of the best), travel is one of the most appealing and delusive. In the world at large everything is in a sorry state; those who won't admit so, feel it as profoundly and bitterly as those who assert it. However, divine hope is always there, pursuing its purpose in our humble hearts, and ever inspiring us with that yearning for the best, that ceaseless search for the ideal.

An ordered society, which cannot even rely on the sympathy of those who support it, satisfies no one, and each of us goes his own particular way. One individual embraces art, another buries himself in science, and the majority amuse themselves the best they can. All of us, as soon as we have the opportunity and the money, travel, or rather we escape, for the important thing is not so much to travel, as to get away. Do you understand me? Which one of us hasn't some grief to forget or some yoke to throw off? No one.

Anyone who isn't completely absorbed in his work, or benumbed by laziness, is incapable, I assure you, of staying for a long time in the same place without becoming unhappy and without desiring a change. If someone is successful (and one has to be very great or very mean to be so today), he imagines that travelling will add something to his good fortune. Lovers and newly-weds set off for Switzerland or Italy, the same as the idle and hypochondriacs. In a word, whoever feels the necessity to be alive or to fade away is possessed of the restlessness of the wandering Jew, and goes as soon as possible to some distant place to look for a love-nest, or a secluded spot wherein to die.

God forbid that I should declaim against people moving about, and that I should envisage a future with men tied to their country, their lands and their homes, like polyps on a sponge! But if intelligence and morality are to progress simultaneously with the development of commerce, it seems to me that the railways are not designed merely to transport from one point on the globe to another persons suffering from an attack of the "blues", or consumed with an unhealthy malaise.

I would like to imagine the human race as happier, and therefore more tranquil and enlightened, living two sorts of lives; one, sedentary, characterized by domestic bliss, civic duties, studious meditation, philosophic contemplation; the other, active, involving honourable relationships which would replace the shameful business we call trade, artistic inspiration, scientific research, and above all, the propagation of ideas. Briefly, I think the normal object of travelling is the need for making fresh contacts and congenial intercourse, and that pleasure should always be combined with duty. On the contrary, however, I believe that the majority of us travel nowadays in search of mystery and isolation, spurred on by a kind of resentment which the society of our fellow men produces on our outlook on life, be it easygoing or toilsome.

In regard to myself, I set out in order to satisfy a desire for rest and quiet, of which I was feeling in particular need at that time. As there is not time for everything in the world we have fashioned for ourselves, I supposed once more that, if I searched well, I would find some remote, noiseless retreat where I would not have to write letters, read papers, nor receive visitors; where there would be no necessity to take off my dressing-gown; where the days would only have twelve hours; where I could shed all obligations to society, isolate myself from the intellectual agitation that afflicts us all in France, and where I could devote a year or two to studying a little history, and to learning my language afresh with my children.

Who amongst us has not at some time selfishly dreamed of forsaking his-job, his usual way of life, his relations and even his friends, in order to go and live on some enchanted island, without cares or responsibilities, and above all without newspapers?

It can be said in all seriousness that journalism (the be all and end all of everything, as Aesop would have said) has created for man a completely new life, full of progress, profit and preoccupation. It is humanity's mouthpiece, which comes every morning to tell us when we wake up what people have been doing the day before, proclaiming sometimes great truths, sometimes great lies, but always recounting mankind's every step and recording the acts of the body politic. And, in spite of all the faults and displeasing features which disfigure it, isn't it something rather great?

But at the same time as this is necessary for revealing the general effect of our thoughts and actions, isn't it terrible and shocking to see in all its details how strife has spread everywhere, and how the weeks and months slip by accompanied by discord and outrage, without a single issue being solved, and without any noticeable progress being made? And in this troubled interlude, made all the worse for being so long drawn out in its various phases, don't we artists often feel like letting go of the helm, falling asleep on the deck of the ship, and not waking up until several years have passed, to greet the new land to which we may find ourselves transported?

If this really could be, if we were able to forsake the community and cut ourselves off from all contact with politics for a length of time, we would be astonished when we returned at the progress accomplished during our absence. But this facility has not been granted to us; when we flee from the noise and bustle in search of forgetfulness and quiet among some people who take life more slowly, and whose spirit is not so fervent as ours, we experience there troubles that we had not foreseen, and we regret having left the present for the past, the living for the dead.

That then quite simply is what the theme of my narrative will be, and why I am undertaking the task of writing it, although it gives me little pleasure to do so, and I had intended at the start to keep my personal feelings to myself as much as possible; however, it now seems to me that such laziness would look more like cowardice, and I retract from it.

CHAPTER V

W E arrived in Palma in the month of November in 1838, in a heat comparable to that of the month of June in our country. We had left Paris a fortnight earlier in extremely cold weather. For us it was a great pleasure, after having felt the first touches of winter, to leave the enemy behind us. To this pleasure was added that of looking round a city of great character, which possesses a large number of monuments of the first order in beauty and rarity.

However, difficulty in finding accomodation soon began to worry us, and we realised that our Spanish friends who had recommended Majorca to us as the most hospitable country and the richest in possibilities, had been mistaken as much as we were. In a place so near to the great civilizations of Europe, we couldn't understand why it was not possible to find a single lodging-house. This lack of a hostelry for visitors ought to have warned us from the very first moment what Majorca was like in comparison with the rest of the world, and decided us to return without delay to Barcelona, where at least there is a very poor inn to stop at, ambitiously called the *Fonda de las Cuatro Naciones* (Inn of the Four Nations).

In Palma it is necessary to make reservations several

months in advance with about a score of reputable persons, to whom one has been recommended, to avoid having to sleep in the street. The most that could be done for us was to provide us with two small furnished rooms (or rather, unfurnished), in a kind of low class tavern, where foreigners had to be satisfied with a narrow bedstead and mattress as soft and yielding as a slab of slate, a rush chair, and, in the matter of food, pepper and garlic to taste.

In a very short time we realised that if we didn't show ourselves delighted with this reception, we would be looked at askance, as though we were insolent people or mischief makers, or at least, we would be regarded pityingly as being mentally deficient. Unfortunate is the person who doesn't pretend to be content with everything in Spain! The slightest grimace at finding dirtiness in the beds or scorpions in the soup would cause the most profound scorn and raise general indignation. For this reason we were very careful not to complain, and little by little, we came to understand to what this scarcity of resources and apparent lack of hospitality was due.

Apart from the habitual inertia and lack of energy of the Majorcans, the civil war which had been raging in Spain for a long time had, at that period, severed all communication between the island and the mainland. Majorca had become the refuge for as many Spaniards from the peninsula as it could take; and the natives, intrenched in their homes, had no wish to sally forth in search of adventures or hard knocks in the mother country.

To this must be added the total absence of industries, and the heavy customs tariffs which result in an excessive tax being levied on all goods necessary for the general well-being.[1] Palma can hold only a certain number of inhabitants,

1. For a piano we had sent from France, they demanded seven hundred francs import duty; it was almost the value of the instrument. We wanted to return it, but that wasn't allowed. To leave it in the port pending further instructions was forbidden. To have it brought into the town by a different route (we were living in the country) to avoid toll charges, which are different from customs duty, was against the law. To leave it in the town in order to avoid exit charges, which

54

and according as the population increases, the people have to crowd together a little more. No renovations take place in the houses. Except perhaps in the case of two or three families, the furniture has changed little during the last two hundred years. They know nothing about the modern style, luxurious living, nor the comforts of life. There is apathy, but there are difficulties also; and so they remain. They have the bare necessities of life, but nothing over; hence their hospitality goes no further than words.

There is a hallowed expression in Majorca, as in all Spain, which excuses them from parting with anything. It consists actually in offering you everything: *La casa y todo lo que hay en ella está a su disposición* (The house and all that's in it is at your disposal). A picture cannot be admired, a cloth touched, a chair raised without someone saying in all affability: *Es a la disposición de usted* (It is at your disposal). But you must guard against accepting even a pin, for it would be a gross indiscretion.

Shortly after my arrival in Palma, I committed an imprudent error of this kind, which I think the Marquis[2] will never forgive me. I had been strongly commended to this young Palma nobleman, and I thought I could accept the offer of the loan of his carriage to go for a drive. He had offered it to me with so much kindness! But the next day a note from the marquis made me realise that I had contravened all the proprieties. I hastened to send the carriage back to him without having made use of it.

Nevertheless, I have met exceptions to this rule, but it was a question of individuals who had travelled, and as a result could be considered as men of the world. If any other persons felt themselves under an obligation to help us, none of them (and I must say this to show the penury to which

---

are different from entry charges, also couldn't be done. To hurl it into the sea was the best thing we could have done with it, if we'd had the right to. After a fortnight's arguing we managed to take it out of the city through one particular gate rather than other, and we settled the business for some four hundred francs.

2. Marquis of la Bastida.

the island was reduced on account of the customs restrictions and lack of industries) could have lent us a corner in his house without inflicting on himself such trouble and privation that it would, in truth, have been very wrong of us to accept it. All these difficulties became very obvious to us when we were looking for a place wherein to settle ourselves. In the whole city it was impossible to find a single apartment that was habitable.

A dwelling in Palma consists of four absolutely bare walls, without doors or windows, only openings. In the majority of the middle-class houses, glass panes are not used; and when they want to avail themselves of this luxury, which is very necessary in winter, they have to order window frames to be made. Every tenant on leaving (but they hardly ever move) takes away with him the window-sashes, the locks and even the hinges of the doors. His successor is obliged to replace them, unless he prefers to live in the open air, a custom which is certainly very prevalent in Palma.

Well now; six months are necessary to manufacture not only doors and windows, but also beds, tables, chairs and any piece of furniture, however simple and primitive it may be. There are very few workmen, and those that there are never hurry, and lack tools and materials. There is always a good reason for the Majorcan not to get a move on. There's lots of time, life is long! One has to be French, that is to say, mad and extravagant, to want something to be done at once. And if you've waited six months, why not wait another six months? If you don't like the country, why stay in it? Do the islanders want you here? They can do very well without the presence of foreigners. Do you think you've come here to turn everything upside down? You certainly won't!

"But have you nothing we can hire?"

"Hire? What's this about hiring furniture? Do you think we have surplus furniture for hire?"

"Then why isn't there any for sale?"

"For sale? For that we would have to carry a stock, and do you think we can afford to make furniture that hasn't been ordered? If you're in such a hurry, have it sent from France, since it seems they have everything in that country."

"But to order it from France we would have to wait at least six months, and pay duty on it. So then, when one commits the folly of coming here, is to go away the only remedy?"

"That's what I would advise. On the other hand, have patience, lots of patience. *Mucha calma* (keep perfectly calm); that is a sound Majorcan saying."

We were about to put this advice into practice, and certainly very willingly, when someone did us the doubtful favour of letting us a house in the country.

It was the country seat of a rich citizen, who let us have it with all its furniture at, for us, a very moderate rent, but which would be considered high enough by the Majorcans.[3] It was furnished like all villas in the country: it had folding or wooden beds painted green, some consisting of two trestles on which two planks were placed and a thin mattress; rush chairs and tables of unplaned wood; bare walls well whitewashed and, a most exceptional luxury, glass windows in almost every bedroom; finally, by way of decoration, in the room which was supposed to be the lounge, four horrible, ornate fire-screens, like those which are usually seen in our most wretched village taverns, and which our landlord, *Señor Gómez,* had had the ingenuousness to put into frames as if they were valuable engravings. For the rest the house was spacious, airy, in fact too airy, well laid out, and built in a very picturesque place at the foot of a fertile hill slope, and in a rich valley from where one could see the yellow walls of Palma, the huge mass of the cathedral, and the sea sparkling on the horizon.

Enticed by lovely weather and delightful scenery, which was quite new to us, the first few days that we passed in this rural retreat went by in pleasant walks and rambles.

I have never been very far from my homeland, although I have spent a large part of my life travelling. It was there-

3.   About one hundred francs a month. *(Translator's note.)*

57

fore the first time that I was seeing vegetation and country completely different from that found in our temperate latitudes. When I went to Italy, I landed on the coast of Tuscany, and the grandiose ideas I had formed of that region prevented me appreciating its pastoral beauty and smiling grace. On the borders of the Arno, I might as well have been on the banks of the Indre;[4] and I arrived in Venice without being surprised at or stirred by anything I was seeing for the first time. But in Majorca I couldn't make any comparison with other places I had known before; the men, the houses, the plants, and even the small pebbles on the road had a different and special character. My children were so taken with them that they collected a lot and endeavoured to fill our trunks with the beautiful quartz and marble stones streaked with every colour, of which the dry stone walls that fence in the gardens and fields are composed. On this account the peasants, when they saw us gathering even the dead branches, took us either for apothecaries or plain imbeciles.

4. A river in central France.

CHAPTER VI

THE island owes the great contrasts in its scenery both to the terrestrial upheavals that have taken place since the world began, and to the ever-changing scene presented by widely cultivated ground. From the place where we were living at that moment, called Establiments, the extensive horizon of several miles offered a very varied panorama.

All around us the cultivated land was arranged in terraces, irregularly laid out on the hillsides. This system of cultivation in terraces, which is adopted in all parts of the island under the constant threat of heavy rains and sudden floods in the water-courses, favours the growth of trees, and gives to the countryside the aspect of a well kept orchard.

To our right, the hills rose progressively in gentle slopes from the pasture land to the pine-covered heights. At the foot of these mountains there is a water-course down which a torrent pours in winter and in the sudden heavy showers of summer; but when we arrived it looked like a disorderly bed of pebbles.

But the beautiful moss which covered the stones — the small bridges coated green by the humidity, with fissures in places caused by the violence of the current, and half hidden by the hanging branches of the willows and poplars — the intertwining of these lovely, slender, leafy trees, which leaned over to form an archway of greenness from one bank to the other — a thin trickle of water which flowed silently among the reeds and myrtles — and often a group of women and children, with their goats, squatting in some quiet backwater — all make this place a wonderful subject for a picture. Every day we went for a walk along the bed of the torrent, and we called this nook the "Poussin", for such an uncumbered, unspoilt and wild piece of nature reminded us by its gravity of the great master's favourite landscapes.

A few hundred steps from our house the torrent divided into several branches, and its course seemed to become lost in the low-lying country. The olive and carob trees united their branches above the tilled land and gave this cultivated region the appearance of a wood.

On the many hills that border this wooded district there are several cottages built in quite an imposing, typical style, despite their truly Lilliputian size. It is impossible to surmise how many barns, cart-sheds, cattle-sheds, farm-yards and gardens a *pagès* (peasant freeholder) gradually acquires in about an acre and a half of land, and what innate preasure he unconsciously takes in this whimsical collection. The cottage usually consists of two stories with a flat roof, whose projecting edge gives shade to a very exposed verandah, like the tier of battlements which surmount a Florentine house-top. This symmetrical finish lends an appearance of grandeur and strength to the most fragile and poorest buildings. The enormous bunches of corn-cobs hanging down from each opening in the verandah to dry off in the air, form a festoon of colour that alternates between red and yellow amber, whose effect is incredibly pleasing.

Around each cottage there generally stands a thick hedge of cactus or prickly-pear, whose extraordinary leaves entwine forming a wall, which keeps the wind off the frail shelters made of reeds and canes that serve as sheepfolds. As stealing from each other is unheard of among these country people, they only use barriers of this kind to enclose their properties. A few plantations of almond and orange trees surround the

60

market garden, where peppers and tomatoes are almost exclusively grown; but all this is of a wonderful colour, and often, to crown the beautiful picture which the place makes, a solitary palm tree unfurls its magnificent, parasol-like foliage, or bends over with the equal gracefulness of a handsome plume of feathers.

This region is one of the most prosperous in the island, and the reasons for it which Grasset de Saint-Sauveur gives in his "Journey to the Balearic Isles" confirm what I have said regarding the insufficiency of the agriculture in general in Majorca. The observations that this government official made in 1807 about the apathy and ignorance of the Majorcan country-folk led him to investigate the causes; and he found two basic ones.

The first was the large number of monasteries which at that time absorbed part of the population, which in any case was anything but dense. This obstacle has disappeared thanks to Mendizabal's energetic decree, for which the devout and pious Majorcans will never forgive him.

The second was the spirit of servitude that prevailed among the people, and which confined them by the dozen to the service of the rich and of the nobility. This bad practice still subsists in full force. Every Majorcan aristocrat has a large domestic staff which he strives to maintain on his limited income, despite the fact that he gets little benefit from them. It is impossible to be worse served than he is by this sort of honorary servant. When the question is asked on what a rich Majorcan can spend his money, in a country where there are no luxuries nor temptations of any kind, it is impossible to answer unless one has seen his house, full of scruffy idlers of both sexes, who occupy a part of the building allotted to them for their quarters, and who, after spending a year in their master's service, have acquired a lifelong right to a home, clothing and maintenance. Those who wish to leave the service can do so foregoing some of their privileges, but custom still allows them to go every morning to have a cup of chocolate with their old companions and,

61

like Sancho in Camacho's house, to participate in all the gala meals of the household.

At first sight, these customs seem to be patriarchal, and one feels inclined to admire the republican sentiment which governs such relations between master and servant; but immediately one notices that this is a republicanism after the style of ancient Rome, and that these servants are chained by laziness or penury to the extravagant will of their lordly employers. In Majorca it is a wasteful luxury to have fifteen servants in a house where two would be enough. And when you can see vast stretches of land untilled, industry abandoned, and all progress proscribed by ineptitude and negligence, you don't know whom to blame, whether the master who encourages and perpetuates in this way the moral abasement of his fellow-beings, or the slave, who prefers a degrading idleness to work, which would give him an independence consistent with human dignity.

However, on account of the increase in their budget of expenses and the decrease in their revenue, it has occurred that some rich Majorcan property owners have decided to remedy the slackness of their tenant farmers and the scarcity of labour. They have sold part of their lands to their workers on a lease-hold for life basis, and Grasset de Saint-Sauveur has confirmed that, on all the big properties where this system has been introduced, apparently barren ground has produced so much in the hands of men determined to improve it, that in a few years many of them had prospered substantially.

Grasset's predictions have been realised completely, and today the district of Establiments, among others, has become a huge garden. The population has increased, a large number of houses have been built on the rising ground, and the country people have achieved a certain affluence which, if it hasn't yet fully taught them a lesson, at least has given them a greater taste for work. Many more years will be necessary before the Majorcan becomes energetic and hard-working; and if, like us, he goes through the painful stage of yearning to get rich quick, and succeeds finally in understanding that that is not the sole purpose of life, we can well leave him to pass the time with his guitar and his rosary.

But, doubtless, a better fate than ours in reserved for these young countries, which one day we will initiate into true civilization without reminding them too much of all that we have done for them. They are not yet sufficiently mature to face up to the revolutionary storms that our striving after perfection has brought down on our heads. Alone, condemned, mocked at, and opposed by the rest of the world, we have made enormous strides, and the noise of our gigantic struggles has not awakened from their slumber these small communities who sleep within range of our guns in the midst of the Mediterranean. However, the day will come when we will bestow on them the baptism of liberty, and they will sit at the banquet like "the labourers from the fields at the twelfth hour". Let us find a slogan for our social destiny, let us realise our sublime dreams, and while neighbouring countries gradually come into our revolutionary diocese, these unfortunate islanders, whose weakness puts them at the mercy of predatory nations, will join our fellowship.

Until that day when we shall be the first in Europe to proclaim the law of equality for all men and independence for all peoples, the ruling factors in the world will be either the "force majeure" of militarism, or the subtle power of those most versed in the game of diplomacy. The rights of the people is only a phrase, and the fate of all small, isolated countries,

like the Transylvanian, the Turk and Hungarian,[1]

is to be swallowed up by the conqueror. If it must always be like this, I would wish neither Spain, England, nor even France to be the tutelary nation of Majorca; and I would be as little interested in its fortuitous future as in the novel civilization we are introducing into Africa.

Author's Note
1. La Fontaine, the Fable of *The Thieves and the Ass*.

One of the personages who made the journey to Majorca: Maurice son of George Sand.

Another personality of the journey: the mischievous Solange, daughter of George Sand.

CHAPTER VII

W E had been three weeks in Establiments when the rains
began. Up to then we had had unsurpassable weather. The
lemon trees and the myrtles were still in flower, and during
the first days of December I stayed out in the open on the
terrace until five o'clock in the early morning, enjoying the
delightful temperature. You can believe me when I say this,
for I know nobody in the world who is more sensitive to
cold than I am, and enthusiasm for nature is incapable of
rendering me insensible even to the slightest chilliness. On
the other hand, in spite of the fascination of the scenery illuminated by the moon and of the perfume of the flowers
which reached even me, my night vigil didn't profoundly stir
me. I was there, not as a poet in search of inspiration, but as
a mere idler who looks and listens. I remember that I occupied the time picking out the noises of the night and trying to
identify them.

It is very true, and everyone knows it, that each country
has its own harmonies, its own discords, its cries, its mysterious ripples of sound; and these characteristic, external manifestations are what generally impress the traveller most.
The lapping of the water against the cold, marble walls, the
slow and measured steps of the policemen on the quay, the

sharp and almost childlike squeak of the shrewmice chasing each other on the muddy flagstones, in short, all the furtive, peculiar noises which disturb the silence of the Venetian nights, are nothing like the monotonous sound of the sea, the *¿quién vive?* (who goes there?) of the sentries, and the melancholy chant of the *serenos* (night-watchmen), in Barcelona. Lake Maggiore has a very different atmosphere to that of the Lake of Geneva. The constant cracking of the pine cones in the woods of Switzerland in no way resembles the cracking that one hears on the glaciers.

In Majorca the silence is deeper than anywhere else. The she-donkeys and the mules, who spend the night grazing, sometimes break it when they shake their cattle bells, whose sound is not so low and is more melodious than those carried by the Swiss cows. The music of the bolero can be heard in the most solitary places and on the darkest nights; for there isn't a countryman who doesn't have his guitar, and who doesn't take it with him everywhere and at all hours. From my terrace I could also hear the sea, but so eak and distant that the strangely fantastic and alluring poetry of the Djinns came back to my memory:

J'ecoute,	I listen,
Tout fuit.	Everything flees.
On doute,	One hesitates,
La nuit,	at night,
Tout passe;	everything passes away;
L'espace	Distance
Efface	effaces
Le bruit.	noise.

In the farmhouse nearby I heard the crying of a child, and the mother, to send it to sleep, sang a beautiful ballad of the country, rather monotonous and very sad, and Arabic in tone. But other less poetic voices came to remind me of the grotesque side of Majorca.

The pigs woke up and started to grunt in a way I couldn't describe. Then the *pagès,* father of the family, also woke up

at the sound of his beloved pigs, as the mother had awakened too beforehand at the crying of her child. I noticed that
the man put his head out of the window and reprimanded the
lodgers in the pig-sty in a very authoritative voice. The pigs
seemed to understand him perfectly, for they fell silent. After
this, the *pagès,* probably to induce sleep again, began to tell
his beads in a doleful voice, which fell and rose according as
sleep came over him or was dispelled, like the distant murmur of the waves. From time to time the pigs would still let
out savage grunts; then the *pagès* would raise his voice a little without interrupting his prayer, and the docile animals,
quietened by an *ora pro nobis* or an *Ave María* pronounced
in a certain manner, would suddenly become dumb. As for
the infant, doubtlessly it was listening with its eyes open,
sunk in that kind of stupor into which incomprehensible
noises plunge the dawning mind of man in the cradle, which
works so mysteriously before revealing itself.

But all at once like an epilogue, after a succession of
cloudless, serene nights, it began to pour with rain. One
morning, after the wind had disturbed us all night with its
long drawn-out howls while the rain drummed against the
window-panes, we heard, on waking up, the noise of the
torrent which was beginning to make its way through the
stones in the river-bed. The next day, the noise became
much louder; and two days later the water was rolling the
boulders in its path over and over. The flowers had all fallen
from the trees, and the rain was dripping into our badly
ceiled rooms.

One cannot understand why the Majorcans take such little precautions against the force of the wind and the rain.
Their self-deception or blatant indifference in this respect is
so great, that they completely deny the very existence of
these occasional but most unpleasant inclemencies of their
climate. Even after two months of deluge which we had to
put up with, they maintained that it never rained in Majorca.
If we had taken better notice of the position of the mountain
peaks and the usual direction of the wind, we would have

realised well beforehand what unavoidable discomforts lay before us.

But another disillusionment was still reserved for us, and it is one which I have already referred to when I began this account of my final journey. One of our party fell ill. Being of very delicate constitution, and suffering greatly from an irritation of the larynx, he soon began to feel the effects of the dampness. *La Casa del Viento* (The House of the Wind, or *Son Vent* in the Majorcan language), which was the name of the villa that *Señor Gómez* had let to us, became uninhabitable. The walls were so thin that the lime with which our bedrooms had been whitewashed swelled like a sponge. I have never felt the cold so badly, although actually the weather wasn't too chilly. But for us, who are used to warming ourselves in winter, that house without any fireplace was like a blanket of ice on our backs, and I felt frozen stiff.

We could not get accustomed to the asphyxiating smell of the braziers, and our invalid began to suffer and to cough. From that moment we became an object of horror and fear to the villagers. We were accused and convicted of pulmonary consumption, which was equivalent to the plague according to the prejudices of the Spanish medical world against contagion. A wealthy doctor who, for the modest sum of forty-five francs, condescended to visit us, declared that it was nothing, and prescribed nothing. We gave him the nickname of *Malvavisco* (marsh mallow), because that was all he could suggest.

Another doctor came obligingly to our aid, but the pharmacy in Palma was so lacking that we could only get horrible drugs. Besides, the illness got worse due to causes which neither science nor care could combat properly.

One morning when we were feeling very depressed by the persistence of the rain and by our other worries, we received a letter from the frightful Gomez telling us, in the Spanish fashion, that we had a person with us afflicted with a complaint that was likely to infect his house, and prove a source of danger to his family; by virtue of this he begged us to get out of his place as soon as possible.

68

Such a request did not cause us much displeasure, for we couldn't remain where we were without risk of being drowned in our rooms; but our invalid was in no condition to be moved without danger, especially bearing in mind the means of transport used in Majorca and the state of the weather. Besides, there was the difficulty of not knowing where to go for, as news of our consumptive spread like a flash, we were unable to find lodging for a single night anywhere, not for love of gold. But for the hospitality of the French consul, who performed miracles in order to shelter us under his own roof, we would have been obliged to take refuge in some cavern, like real gypsies.

Another miracle happened; we found an asylum for the winter. There was in the Cartuja (Carthusian monastery) of Valldemosa a Spanish refugee, who had gone into hiding there for some unknown political motive. We had already visited the Cartuja, and we had been surprised at his cultured manners, the melancholy beauty of his wife, and the rustic furniture of their cell, which was quite comfortable nevertheless. The poetic atmosphere of the monastery had driven me to distraction. It came about that the mysterious couple wished to leave the country hurriedly, and they appeared to be prepared to hand over their cell to us with as much pleasure as we had in accepting it. For the fair sum of a thousand francs we acquired, then, a complete set of furniture, but of the sort we could have got in France for a hundred; so rare, costly, and difficult to come by are items of prime necessity in the island.

As we spent four days in Palma, during which I scarcely left the fireplace which the consul was fortunate to possess (the deluge still came down), I will make a digression here in my story to describe briefly the capital of Majorca.

Laurens, who came the next year to explore and sketch its most beautiful features, will be the cicerone that I shall now introduce to the reader, for he is far more versed than I am in archaeology.

PART II

CHAPTER I

ALTHOUGH Majorca was occupied by the Moors for four centuries, few traces of their sojourn have been preserved. In Palma there is only a small bath-house left as a reminder.

Of the Romans there is no trace at all, and of the Carthaginians only a few ruins near the old capital, Alcudia, and the tradition of the birth of Hannibal, which Grasset de Saint-Sauveur attributes to simple Majorcan presumption, although this occurrence is not lacking in probability.[1]

However, the Arabic style has been perpetuated in the lesser buildings in the island, and it has been necessary for Laurens to correct all the archaeological mistakes of his predecessors, so that ignorant visitors, like myself, shouldn't think they were authentic remains of Arab architecture at every step.

"I have not seen in Palma", says Laurens, "any buildings whose date of construction appears to be very ancient. The most interesting by reason of their architecture and antiquity

---

1. The Majorcans claim that Hamilcar, when he was on his way from Africa to Catalonia with his wife, who was pregnant, stopped at a point in the island where there was a temple dedicated to Lucina (goddess of light), and that Hannibal was born there. This story occurs also in the *History of Majorca* by Dameto. (Grasset de Saint-Sauveur.)

all date from the beginning of the 16th century; but the graceful and brilliant art of that period is not revealed there in the same way as in France.

The houses only have one story above the ground-floor, and a very low loft.[2] The entrance from the street is through a porch or rounded archway without any embellishment; but its size and the number of stones arranged radially like long spokes give it an attractive aspect. The light enters the large rooms of the first story through high windows, partitioned by extremely slender columns, which give them a wholly Arabic appearance.

This feature is so pronounced that I have found it necessary to examine more thant twenty houses built in an identical manner, and study all the characteristics of their construction, in order to be certain that these windows had not been removed from one of those really fantastic Arab palaces of which, like the Alhambra in Granada, we have some specimens still remaining.

Only in Majorca have I found columns which, with a height of six feet, are not more than three inches in diameter. The fineness of the marble of which they are made, and the style of the capital which crowns them, led me to suppose that they were of Arabic origin. Although this may not be so, the look of these windows is as graceful as it is original.

The loft which constitutes the top floor is a gallery, or rather, a series of windows placed very close together, which are exact copies of those which ornament the upper part of the Lonja. A very projecting roof, supported by artistically carved beams, protects this last floor from the rain and sun, and creates singular lighting effects with the long shadows it casts on the house, and by the contrast of the brown mass of the structure with the brilliant hues of the sky against which it is outlined.

The stairs, fashioned in great artistic style, rise from a courtyard in the centre of the house, which is separated from

2. They are not really lofts, but more drying-rooms, called "porxos" locally. (Translator's note.)

the entrance onto the stree by a vestibule, where one observes pilasters whose tops are decorated with sculptured leaves or with some nobleman's coat of arms held up by angels.

For more than a century after the Renaissance, the Majorcans lavished money on the building of their private houses. Whilst always following the same general layout, they carried out alterations to the vestibules and stairways according to the architectural changes in style of the times. For this reason Tuscan or Doric columns are to be found everywhere; and the flights of stairs and balustrades give an appearance of costly richness to the mansions of the aristocracy.

This predilection for the ornamentation of the stairways and memento of Arabic art are found also in the most humble dwellings, even where a single flight of steps leads straight from the street to the first floor. Then each stair is covered over with earthenware tiles, adorned with flowers, generally blue or red."

The foregoing description by Laurens is a very accurate one, and the author's drawings show the elegance of these interiors perfectly. Their peristyle would form a beautiful decoration of great simplicity for our theatres.

The paved courtyards, which are sometimes surrounded with columns like the *cortile* of Venetian palaces, generally have a well in the middle of a very simple construction. They have neither the same aspect, nor are they put to the same use as our dirty, bare patios. The entrance to the stables or to the coach-houses never leads off them. They are proper patios, which recall the atrium of the Romans; the wells in the middle evidently occupy the place of the ancient *impluvium*.

When these courtyards are ornamented with flower-pots and small reed mats, they have an appearance that is both elegant and severe at the same time, whose poetical quality is not in the least appreciated by their Majorcan owners, who never cease apologizing for the antiquity of their residences; and if you admire the artistic style they smile, thinking you are making fun of them or perhaps secretly scorning this ridiculous excess of courtesy of the French.

However, you should not imagine that whatever you find in the houses of the Majorcan nobility is equally poetic. There are certain details of uncleanliness which I could not describe to my readers unless, as Jaquemont did when writing about Indian customs, I finished my writing in Latin.

Not knowing Latin, I refer anyone interested to the passage which Grasset de Saint-Sauveur, a less serious writer than Laurens but very accurate on this point, devotes to the position of the larders in many old houses in Spain and Italy. What he writes is very surprising, due to a certain prescription issued by the Spanish medical faculty which is still in full force in Majorca, and which is extremely strange.

The interior of these palaces does not correspond at all to their exterior, and nothing can be more significantly revealing, both from a collective and individual point of view, than the layout and furnishing of residences and apartments. In Paris, for example, where the whims of fashion and the abundance of industrial products bring about startling differences in the look of one dwelling from another, it is enough to enter a well-to-do person's house in order, after a glance round, to form an idea of his character: whether he or she is a peerson of taste and orderliness, miserly or extravagant, of a methodical or romantic spirit, hospitable, or just fond of ostentation. I have my own ideas about this, as everyone else has his; of course that doesn't prevent me frequently making mistakes in my deductions, as generally happens with many other people also.

I have a particular horror of a room that is sparsely furnished and austerely tidy. Unless it is someone highly intellectual and deep-thinking, and quite impervious to external material influences, who inhabits it as though it were a kind of tent, I imagine the occupier of such a room as being empty-headed and cold-hearted. When one really has to live between four walls, I cannot understand why he or she doesn't feel the urge to fill the place with things, be they only knickknacks and bits-and-pieces, and to have something living around, like a bird in a cage, or a vase of carnations.

Empty space and still life freeze me with dread, and symmetry and strict orderliness fill me with gloom; and if I try to imagine what eternal damnation means to me, my hell would be to have to live for ever in one of those provincial houses where order reigns supreme, where nothing changes its place, where nothing is dragged along the floors, where nothing wears out or is broken, and where there is never a bird, dog or a cat, under the pretext that animals damage the furniture. Perish all carpets in the world if I can only have one provided a child or a kitten doesn't play about on it!

This rigid cleanliness does not proceed from a true love of tidiness, but rather from an excessive laziness or a miserly sense of economy. With little more care and energy, a good housewife according to my ideas can keep her house as clean as I insist on keeping my own. But what can one say and think of the customs and ideas of people whose homes are empty and lifeless, with no reason or pretext for extreme tidiness? And if it is easy to be mistaken, as I said a little while ago, in one's assessment of individuals, it is difficult to be so in a general sense. The character of a people is revealed in their clothes and in their furnishings, as much as in their features and language.

I went into a great number of houses going round Palma looking for rooms. They looked so much alike that I could only imagine a general similarity in the character of the occupants. I never entered one of these homes without feeling myself overcome with vexation if not anger, simply by the sight of the bare walls, the dusty, stained flagstones, and the sparse and dirty furniture. Everything bore witness to indifference and inaction. I never saw a book, or woman's handiwork; the men don't read, and the women don't even sew. The only indication of a domestic occupation is the smell of garlic, denoting culinary activities; and the only signs of entertainment are the cigar ends scattered about the floor.

This absence of intellectual life turns the house into something dead and empty, which has nothing in common with our way of life, and makes the Majorcan appear more like an African than a European.

Thus, all these dwellings, where generation succeeds generation without changing anything or leaving its stamp on things which normally form part of our lives in some way or other, seem to me more similar to resting places for caravans than proper houses. And whilst ours give the impression of being real family homes, these places have the appearance of lodging-houses where groups of wandering people assemble to spend the night. Persons who know Spain well have told me that in general the same thing happens in the whole of the peninsula.

As I have already said, the peristyle or *atrium* of the palaces of the *caballeros* (which is what the Majorcan nobility are still called) has a definite atmosphere of hospitality and even of comfort. But, after surmounting the elegant staircase and entering the house, it seems that you have gone into a place designed only for the *siesta:* huge rooms, usually quadrangular in shape, with very high ceilings, very cold, very gloomy, completely bare, whitewashed, with large old family portraits, obscure and placed in line, but so high up you can't distinguish them; four or five greasy leather chairs, eaten with insects, edged with thick, gilt tacks which have not been cleaned for two hundred years; a few mats, or ordinary long-haired sheepskins, thrown here and there on the floor; windows located very high up from the floor and covered with big, heavy curtains; wide doors of black Spanish oak, the same as the panelled ceiling, and sometimes an old cloth of gold door curtain, which shows the family's coat of arms, richly embroidered but tarnished and worn out by time; such are the interiors of the Majorcan palaces. No tables are to be seen except those to eat off. Mirrors are so rare and take up such little space on the immense walls that they reflect nothing.

One usually finds the master of the house standing and smoking in silence, and his wife sitting in an armchair, playing with her fan and thinking about nothing. The children are never on view; they live with the servants, in the kitchen or in the attic, I don't know which. A chaplain visits the house and goes away without doing anything. The twenty or thirty menials have a siesta, while a grumbling old female domestic answers the door after the caller has rung the bell for the fifteenth time.

This sort of life certainly doesn't lack character, as we would say in the very wide range of meaning that we give to this word these days; but if the most peaceable of our citizens was condemned to live that way, he would go mad with despair, or become a demagogue through spiritual reaction.

The background of the port of Palma as seen by George Sand and Frederick Chopin in October 1838.
(Lithograph by Muntaner, 1840).

The promenade known as the Borne in Palma, in the days when George Sand was in Majorca.
(Lithograph by Muntaner, 1840)

CHAPTER II

The three principal buildings in Palma are: the cathedral, the Lonja, and the Palacio Real.

The cathedral, attributed by the Majorcans to James the Conqueror, their first Christian king and in a certain way their Charlemagne, was in fact commenced during his reign, but wasn't finished until 1601. It is of stark severity; and the limestone of which it is constructed throughout is of a very fine grain and of a beautiful amber colour.

This imposing mass, which rises up from the edge of the sea, produces a great effect as one enters the harbour; but, in reality, the only remarkable feature about it is the southern portal, described by Laurens as the most beautiful example of Gothic architecture that he has ever had the opportunity to draw. The edifice has a most austere and sombre interior.

As the wind off the sea came in with full force through the openings on the southern face of the building, especially through the main entrance, knocking down pictures and sacred vessels during the services, all doorways and windows on this side were closed up.

The central nave measures 540 *palmos* (approx. 340 feet)

81

6

in length, by 375 (approx. 250 feet) in width.[1] In the middle of the choir there is a marble sarcophagus, quite plain, which is opened to show visitors the mummy of King James II, the son of the Conqueror, a devout prince, as weak and gentle as his father was bold and bellicose.[2]

The Majorcans claim that their cathedral is very superior to Barcelona's, in the same way as, according to them, their Lonja is infinitely more beautiful than the one in Valencia. I have not been able to confirm the latter assertion; but in regard to the former, it cannot be upheld. In both cathedrals there is to be seen the singular token and reminder, which is to be found in most of the archiepiscopal churches in Spain; namely, the loathly painted, wooden head of a Moor, surmounted by a turban, which crowns the lower part of the organ ornamentation. This image of a cut-off head, which sometimes has a long white beard, is painted red below to represent the unchaste blood spilled by the conquered one.[3]

Coats of arms are displayed on the keystones of the arches in the aisles. To have their escutcheons in the House of God was a privilege for which the Majorcans paid highly, and thanks to this impost on their vanity, the cathedral was able to be completed in a century in which religious zeal had cooled down somewhat. However, we must not be unfair to the extent of attributing only to the Majorcans a shortcoming that was common to the supposedly pious nobility of the entire world at that time.

The Lonja is the monument that impressed me most, by its graceful proportions and its character of originality, which have omitted neither perfect symmetry nor stylish simplicity.

This Exchange was begun and finished in the first half of the fifteenth century. The illustrious Jovellanos described it in great detail, and it was illustrated by a very interesting

1. The Spanish *palmo* is equivalent to the pam of our French southern provinces. (*Author's note.*)
2. In 1947 the mummy was moved to the chapel of the Trinity, at the back of the presbytery, and placed in one of the royal sarcophagi fashioned by Frederick Marés. (*Translator's note.*)
3. As far as I know, there has never been a Moor's head in Palma Cathedral. (*Translator's note.*)

sketch in the *Semanario Pintoresco* (Weekly Graphic Magazine), published many years ago. The interior is a vast hall, whose arched roof is supported by six columns fluted with elegant subtlety. Intended originally as a meeting place for merchants and the large number of seafairing folk that flocked to the port of Palma, the Lonja testifies to the past splendour of Majorcan commerce; today it is used only for the celebration of public festivals.

It must have been interesting to see the Majorcans, still dressed in the rich costumes of their predecessors, disporting themselves gravely in this antiquated ballroom; but rain kept us captive on the mountain, and it was not possible for us to attend such Carnival entertainments, less celebrated but perhaps less solemn than those of Venice. With regard to the Lonja, lovely as it seemed to me, it has not erased the memories I have kept of that wonderful jewel called the "Cadoro", the ancient Mint situated on the Grand Canal.

The Palacio Real of Palma, which Grasset de Saint-Sauveur doesn't hesitate to qualify as Roman or Moorish (which has inspired him with emotions quite in keeping with Imperial tastes) was built, as he says, in 1309. Laurens expresses doubts concerning the arched windows with central pillars and the puzzling little columns, which he examined in this old structure.

Would it be very rash to attribute the anomalies in style which we find in so many Majorcan buildings to the exploitation of ancient fragments in later constructional work? Just as in France and Italy the Renaissance introduced genuine Greek and Roman medallions and bassreliefs into sculptural ornamentations, isn't it probable that the Christians in Majorca, after destroying all the structures of the Arabs,[4] would

---

4.   The capture and sacking of Palma by the Christians, in December 1229, are very graphically described in Marsigli's chronicle. Here is an extract:

"According to what we are told by Arnaldo de Castellvell, who later became a friar of the order of Preachers, the pillagers, when they entered the houses, found beautiful women and attractive young Moorish girls displaying on their laps gold and silver coins, pearls and precious stones, gold and silver bracelets, necklaces, and every kind of

utilize their rich spoils by incorporating them in the form of decorative work in their new buildings?

Be that as it may, the Palacio Real in Palma has a very picturesque appearance. There is nothing more irregular, more comfortless, or more starkly mediaeval than this lordly abode; but also there is nothing so arrogant, so typical, so nobly impressive as this old edifice, composed of galleries, towers, terraces and archways, one above the other rising to a considerable height, and finished off by a Gothic angel which, from the depth of the clouds, contemplates Spain over the sea.

This palace, which keeps the archives, is the present residence of the Captain-General, the most important personage in the island. This is how Grasset de Saint-Sauveur describes the interior:

"The first apartment is a kind of vestibule which is used as a guardroom. To the right there are two large rooms in which there is scarcely a seat. The third is the audience chamber, graced by a throne of scarlet velvet edged with gold fringes, and placed on a dais three steps up, which is covered with a carpet. On either side there is a lion in gilded wood. The canopy over the throne is also of scarlet velvet, crowned by a crest of ostrich feathers. Above the throne hang portraits of the king and queen. In this room on formal occasions and gala days, the General receives the different bodies of the administration, officers of the garrison, and foreigners of high rank or prominence."

We were carrying letters of introduction to the Captain-

---

valuable jewel. They exposed all these objects to the looks of the armed men who came upon them, and weeping bitterly said to them in Arabic: «Take it all, but spare our lives». The lust for loot and licentious habits were such that the men of the household of the king of Aragon didn't show themselves near him for a week, engrossed as they were in searching for hidden objects which they wanted to appropriate. And so one morning, as neither the cook nor servants of the royal household could be found, an Aragonese nobleman, Ladro, said to the monarch, «Sire, I invite you to eat with me, because they tell me there is a good cow at my place; there you will be able to eat and sleep tonight». The king was very pleased and followed the said nobleman" (*Author's note.*)

General, who exercises the function of governor in the island; and one of us, who undertook to deliver these to him, had the honour in fact of being received in this chamber. Our companion found the high functionary standing near the throne, which was certainly the same one as described by Grasset de Saint-Sauveur in 1807, and which was by now worn, faded, peeling, and somewhat stained with oil and grease. The two lions were no longer gilded, but still preserved the same fierce expression. Only the royal effigy had changed, which was by this time the innocent Isabel; it was a monstrous sort of inn sign, occupying the old gilt frame where her august forbears had succeeded one another rather like the models facing the easel of a pupil in a painting class. The governor, despite being accomodated like the Duke d'Iréneus d'Hoffman, was none the less a person held in high esteem and a very courteous nobleman.

A fourth, very interesting old piece of architecture is the palace of the Town Hall, a work of the 16th century, whose style is compared, with reason, to that of the palaces in Florence. It is remarkable especially for its corbelled roof, which is similar to those of Swiss chalets. But this one in Majorca has the peculiarity of being panelled underneath with richly sculptured rosework in wood, alternating with caryatids or female figures stretched below the corbelling, whose weight they appear to be bearing with suffering, for most of them have their faces hidden in their hands.

I have not seen inside of this edifice, which holds a collection of portraits of Majorca's great men. Among these illustrious personages is the famous Don Jaime, portrayed as the king in a pack of cards; likewise one can see a very old picture of the funeral of the Majorcan, Ramon Llull, which shows as well a very varied and interesting array of the ancient costumes worn by the enlightened doctor's cortège. Finally there is in this municipal building a magnificent "San Sebastian", by Van Dyck, of which nobody in Majorca had told me.

Laurens adds: "Palma possesses an Art School, which has already produced in the present 19th century, thirty-six painters, eight sculptors, eleven architects and six engravers, all of them masters of their craft if we are to believe the *Glossary of Majorca's celebrated artists,* which the learned Antonio Furio has recently published. I frankly confess that during my stay in the island I never had reason to realise I was surrounded by so many distinguished people, for I saw nothing to make me even guess at their existence.

Some wealthy families treasure many pictures of the Spanish school... But if you go through the shops or enter the house of an ordinary citizen, you will only find those same multicoloured illustrations which our hawkers are accustomed to exhibit in our public squares, and which in France can only find a home under the humble roof of the impecunious peasant.

The palace of which Palma is most proud is that of the Count of Montenegro, an aged octogenarian at one time Captain-General, and one of the highest born personages in Majorca as well as one of the most important on account of his wealth. This nobleman has a library which we were permitted to visit; however, I didn't touch a volume (my respect for books almost amounts to fear), and I wouldn't be able to say anything about it if a scholarly compatriot hadn't pointed out to me the importance of the treasures before which I had passed with indifference, like the cockerel among the pearls in the fairy tale.

This fellow countryman,[5] who has stayed more than two years in Catalonia and Majorca in order to carry out studies of the romance languages, has most kindly let me borrow his notes, and authorised me with a generosity rare among erudite folk to make use of them as I like. But I will not do so before warning the reader that this traveller was as much enraptured by things in Majorca as I was disappointed.

I might say, as an explanation of this divergence of impressions, that during my stay the Majorcan population had

5. Monsieur Tastu — one of our must learned linguists, and husband of one of our most talented and noble lady artists. (*Author's note.*)

compressed its living space to make room for twenty thous-
and Spaniards, whom the war had driven into their country;
and without doubt on this account, I found Palma with less
accomodation and the Majorcans less willing than two years
previously to welcome a new influx of foreigners. But I
would rather incur the censure of a friendly disclaimer than
write something that would not represent my true sentiments. Besides, I would prefer to be refuted and admonished
publicly, as I have been privately; for the public would perhaps acquire thereby a book which would be much more accurate and interesting about Majorca than this desultory and
possibly unjust narrative I feel forced to give them.

Let M. Tastu then publish his account of his travels.
I promise him I will read with great gladness anything that
might make me change my opinion of the Majorcans. I have
known some who I would like to be able to think of as re-
presentative of the general type; and who, I hope, will never
doubt my feelings of respect for them, should this script at
any time fall into their hands.

And so, I find in M. Tastu's notes that, among the intellectual riches that Majorca still possesses, there exists this library of the Count of Montenegro, which I went through
with scant reverence escorted by the house chaplain. Really
I was more concerned in examining the interior of the mansion of an elderly, celibate Majorcan nobleman. It was a
gloomy and solemn household, reticently administered by a
priest.

"This library", says Tastu, "has been assembled by the
Count of Montenegro's uncle, Cardinal Despuig, an intimate
friend of Pius VI. The erudite cardinal collected everything
that was notable in bibliography in Spain, France and Italy.
The section that deals with numismatics and the ancient arts
is remarkably complete.

"Among the few manuscripts that are kept there is one
of great interest for enthusiasts of calligraphy or penman-
ship. It is a book of hours with beautiful little illustrations,
drawn in the very best artistic traditions.

"Students of heraldry will find a book on armorial bearings which contains coloured drawings of the coats of arms of the Spanish nobility, including Aragonese, Majorcan, Roussillon and Languedoc families. This writing, which is possibly of the 16th century, belonged to the Dameto family, related by marriage to the Despuig's and the Montenegro's. Turning over the leaves we came across the shield of the Bonapartes, the family from which our great Napoleon was descended, and of which we have a facsimile reproduced further on.

"In addition, there is in this library the beautiful nautical map of the Majorcan, Valseca, a manuscript of 1439, and a masterpiece of calligraphy and topographical drawing, on which the miniature artist has done a wonderful job. This map belonged to Amerigo Vespucci, who bought it for a very high price, as is attested by an inscription of the period on the back of the same: «Questa ampla pelle di geographia fu pagata da Amerigo Vespucci CXXX ducati di oro di marco».

"This precious souvenir of mediaeval geopraphy will be published shortly as a sequel to the Catalan-Majorcan Atlas of 1375, and inserted in volume 14 of the second part of the Notes on the manuscripts of the Academy of Epigraphy and Fine Arts."

My hair stands on end as I transcribe this, because a terrible scene comes to my mind. We were in this same library of Montenegro's, and the chaplain was unfolding before us this very valuable and rare relic of the past, bought by Amerigo Vespucci for a hundred and thirty gold ducats, and for God knows how much by that lover of antiquities, Cardinal Despuig... when it occurred to one of the forty or fifty servants of the house to place a cork inkwell on one of the corners of the parchment to keep it open. And the inkwell was full, full to the brim!

The parchment, accustomed to being folded, or perhaps impelled by some malign influence, twitched, crackled, gave a sudden jump, and then coiled up on itself taking with it the inkwell, which disappeared inside the triumphant roll now sweeping all obstacles aside. There was a general outcry, and the chaplain turned paler than the parchment itself.

The map was slowly unrolled, with everybody nevertheless buoyed up by a vain hope. Alas! The inkwell was empty. The parchment was soaked, and the beautiful painted sovereign miniatures were swimming literally in a sea darker than the Black Sea.

Then everyone lost his head. The servants rushed off and fetched buckets of water, as if they were going to put out a fire, and began to clean up the map with brushes and sponges, intermingling kings, seas, islands and continents. Before we could stop this fatal zeal, the map was in part damaged. But luckily the disfigurement wasn't irremediable; Tastu had made an exact tracing of it, and thanks to him it was possible to repair the damage.

But what must the consternation of the chaplain have been when he had to tell his Lordship about the mishap! We were all about six paces away from the table at the time of the catastrophe; but I am sure that the entire blame would fall on us, and that this deed, brought about by some French people, will not have contributed to our being well received in Majorca.

This grievous event deprived us from admiring other wonders contained in the Montenegro palace: the cabinet of medallions, the old bronzes and the pictures. We hastened to escape before the owner returned and, convinced that he would attribute the damage to us, we didn't dare to return. M. Tastu's notes therefore will make up for my ignorance:

"Next to the cardinal's library there is a cabinet of Celtiberian, Arabic, Roman and mediaeval medallions; an invaluable collection, but now in a lamentable state of disorder, and waiting for some scholastic person to catalogue and classify them.

"The Count of Montenegro's rooms are decorated with works of art of marble or old bronze, which come from the excavations at Ariccia or were bought in Rome by the cardinal. One finds there also many pictures of the Spanish and Italian schools, some of which would not be out of place in the finest galleries of Europe."

I must say something about Bellver Castle, the former

residence of the Majorcan Kings, although I have only seen it from afar, standing on the hill from which it overlooks the sea with great stateliness. It is a very old fortress and one of the harshest state prisons in Spain.

"The ramparts as they are today", says Laurens, "were erected towards the end of the 13th century, and they present in a perfect state of preservation one of the most interesting examples of military architecture in the Middle Ages."

When our traveller visited it, he found there about fifty Carlist prisoners, ragged and almost naked; some of them, almost boys, were happily and noisily eating from bowls of thick macaroni cooked in water. They were being guarded by soldiers who, with cigars in their mouths, were darning their socks.

Actually at that period, it was to Bellver Castle that they transferred prisoners who couldn't be accomodated in the Barcelona prisons, which were overflowing. But more illustrious persons saw its terrible doors shut behind them. Don Gaspar de Jovellanos, one of the most eloquent orators and most powerful writers in Spain, expiated there the transgression of producing his famous pamphlet *Pan y toros* (Bread and bulls), "in the tower of homage, whose dungeon" says Vargas, "is the crudest prison". Jovellanos occupied his gloomy, idle hours in accurately describing his gaol and reconstructing the history of the tragic events of which it had been the scene in the Middle Ages.

The Majorcans also owe to Jovellanos' stay in the island an excellent description of their cathedral and of the Lonja. In a word, his *Letters on Majorca* are the best work that one can consult on the subject.

The same dungeon which Jovellanos had occupied during the parasitic reign of the Prince of Peace, a little later harboured another personage, distinguished in science and politics. This little known story of the life of a man as justly famous in France as Jovellanos was in Spain, is of great interest, because it is one of the most romantic chapters in the life of one whose love for science launched a thousand perilous and stirring adventures.

CHAPTER III

ENTRUSTED by Napoleon with the measuring of the meridian, Arago was in 1808 in Majorca on the mountain known as Clot de Galatzo, when he received the news of the happenings in Madrid and of the removal of Ferdinand. The indignation of the Majorcan people was so great that it was decided to seize and kill the French scientist, and a crowd set off accordingly towards the Clot.

The mountain is situated near the point on the coast where James I landed when he conquered the island from the Moors; and as Arago used to light fires frequently for his own purposes, the Majorcans thought he was making signals to a French squadron with an invasion force.

One of the islanders, called Damian and helmsman of the brigantine that the Spanish government made available for the operation of measuring the meridian, resolved to warn Arago of the danger he was running. Getting ahead of his compatriots, he was able just in time to give him some sailor's clothes with which to disguise himself.

Arago left his mountain at once and hastened to Palma. On the way he ran into those looking for him to do him in, and they asked him about the damned *gabacho* ("Frenchy") they wanted to get rid of. As he spoke the language of the

country very well, Arago answered all his questioners fluent-
ly and he wasn't recognised.

When he got to Palma he went on board the brigantine,
but the skipper, Don Manuel de Vacaro, who up to then had
obeyed his orders, flatly refused to take him to Barcelona;
and the only hiding place he offered him on the vessel wás
a chest which, as Arago found out, was too small for him.

The next day a threatening crowd gathered right on the
water-side, and the captain, Vacaro, informed Arago that he
could not from then on be responsible for his safety; adding
that, in accordance with the advice of the Captain-General,
there was no other way of saving his life than to become a
prisoner in Bellver Castle. For this Captain Vacaro provided
Arago with a boat in which he crossed the bay. The crowd
saw this and rushed off in pursuit, and almost overtook him
at the very moment that the gates of the fortress clanged to
behind his back.

Arago remained two months in his prison, until the Captain-General caused it to be intimated to him that he would
shut his eyes if he wished to get away. He escaped, therefore,
thanks to the help of *Señor Rodríguez,* his Spanish colleague
in the measuring of the meridian.

The same Damian, the Majorcan who had saved his life
on the *Clot de Galatzo,* took him to Algiers in a fishing-boat,
because Arago didn't want to land in either France or Spain
at any price.

During his captivity, Arago was informed by the Swiss
soldiers who were guarding him, that the monks in the island had offered them money to poison him.

In Africa our scientist underwent other vicissitudes,
which he came through also miraculously, but this is nothing to do with our story, and we trust that he himself will
one day write an account of his interesting adventures.

At first sight the Majorcan capital does not reveal its
whole character. Only by roaming through its interior, and
penetrating its deep, mysterious streets at nightfall, can one
appreciate the graceful style and original symmetry of its
most insignificant buildings. But especially when one approa-

ches from the centre of the island and enters by the northern side, does its African aspect become apparent.

Laurens has captured this picturesque beauty which would have escaped an ordinary archaeologist, and has emphasized one of the features which also had stirred me by its grandeur and its solemnity; I am referring to a part of the city wall, not far from the church of San Agustín, where an enormous square mass arises with no other opening in it than a tiny arched door.

A cluster of beautiful palm trees crowns this structure, the last vestige of a fortress of the Knights Templar, wonderful in its melancholy and simplicity, and overlooking the magnificent panorama that starts at the foot of the wall with a smiling, fertile plain and stretches away into the distance as far as the blue mountains of Valldemosa. Towards evening the colour of this landscape varies from hour to hour, harmonising with an increasing intensity. One sunset I saw it coloured a brilliant pink, then it changed to a splendid violet to turn into the colour of silvery lilac and finally, with the approach of night, into a pure, transparent blue.

Laurens has drawn many other landscapes as viewed from the ramparts of Palma; "Every evening" he says, "at the time when the sun colours everything vividly, I used to walk slowly to the walls, stopping at each step to gaze at the lovely effects which the tops of the buildings made against the background of the mountain range or the sea.

"Here the inner slope of the rampart is adorned with a dreadful hedge of aloes from which masses of stalks rise, the arrangement of whose flowers is like a monumental candelabrum; further on there are groups of palm trees in the gardens, together with fig-trees, cactus, orange-trees, and the arborescent castor-oil plant; further on still, balconies and terraces shaded by climbing grape-vines; and finally, the spires of the cathedral, and the belfries and cupolas of the innumerable churches display their silhouettes against the pure, luminous panorama of the sky."

Another walk which roused the same emotions in both Laurens and myself was one I did among the ruins of the

93

monastery of Santo Domingo. At the end of an arbour of very old grapevines supported by marble pillars, four great palm trees can be seen which seem to be enormous on account of the elevation of the terrace on which they are growing. Through their leaves one glimpses the top of the façade of San Esteban,[1] the massive tower of the famous Balearic clock,[2] and the tower with the angel of the Palacio Real.

This monastery of the Inquisition,[3] of which there now only remains a heap of ruins through which some small trees and aromatic plants are pushing their way, has not fallen down owing to the passage of time. Some years ago a swifter

---

1.   The author is probably referring to the tower of the church of Minimos; there is no reference in any ancient chronicle to the existence of a church or tower of San Esteban. *(Translator's note.)*

2.   This clock, which the two mos important historians of Majorca (Dameto and Mut) have described minutely, was still functioning thirty years ago. Grasset de Saint-Sauveur says: "This very old piece of mechanism is called a Sun Clock. It indicates the hours from sunrise to sunset, according to the greater or less extension of the diurnal or nocturnal arc; in such a way that, on the 10th June, it marks the first hour of the day at half past five and the fourteenth at half past seven; the first hour of night at half past eight and the ninth at half past four the following morning. Commencing from the 10th December the reverse happens. During the whole course of the year the hours are accurately regulated according to the changes in sunrise and sunset. This clock is not much use for people in general who rely on modern clocks, but is useful to gardeners in fixing the hours for watering. Where this mechanism came from and when it was brought to Palma are not known. It is assumed it didn't come from Spain, France, Germany or Italy, where the Romans had introduced the custom of dividing the day into twelve hours starting from sunrise. Nevertheless, a priest, the Rector of the University of Palma, in the third part of a work on seraphic religion, affirms that some fugitive Jews recovered this famous clock from the ruins of Jerusalem in the times of Vespasian, and brought it to Majorca where they had taken refuge. This is an extraordinary idea of its origin, but accords with the characterístic propensity of the islanders for everything to do with the .miraculous".

The historian Dameto, and his successor Mut, didn't put the antiquity of the Balearic clock beyond the year 1385. It was bought from the Dominican fathers and placed on the tower where it now is. (Excursion to the Balearic and Pitiusan islands, 1807.) *(Author's note.)*

3.   Improperly so called by George Sand, who is confusing it with the tribunal, doubtless because the chief inquisitors were Dominicans. The tribunal of the Inquisition was installed in a palace situated on the slope of the Teatro, still called by the people the "Inquisitor's slope". *(Translator's note.)*

and more inexorable hand, namely revolution, destroyed and converted into dust this monument which they say was a masterpiece, and whose remains (fragments of rich mosaic and some light arches still standing in the empty space like skeletons) testify to its one-time magnificence.

The destruction of these sanctuaries of catholic art throughout Spain is the cause of great indignation among the Palma aristocracy, and a source of genuine regret for artists. Barely ten years ago perhaps I myself would have been more affected by the vandalism of this devastation than I am now, taking cognizance only of its place in history.

However, although I cannot deplore in the same way that Marliani has done in his Political History of Modern Spain, the weak and at the same time violent aspect of the measures which Mendizabal's decree[4] must have brought with it, yet I confess that among those ruins I felt an emotion very different from the sadness with which such things usually fill me. A thunderbolt had fallen there, and the thunderbolt is a blind instrument, a brutal force, like man's fury; but the law of providence that governs the elements and presides over its apparent disorders well knows that the beginnings of a new life lie hidden in the ashes of its ruins. The day when these monasteries fell, there was in the political atmosphere of Spain something analogous to that instinct for revival which nature experiences after its profuse upheavals.

I don't believe, as people have told me in Palma, that it was only a few malcontents, avid for revenge and plunder, who committed this act of violence under the eyes of a horror-struck populace. A great many malcontents would have been necessary to reduce a mass of buildings to dust in such a manner; and the people too must have been little moved at seeing a highly unpopular decree being carried out in this way.

Rather do I believe that the first stone torn off the top of those cupolas also tore out of the soul of the people a tra-

4. This refers to the decree of disentailment of ecclesiastical properties, carried out by Alvarez Mendizábal, the prime minister of Isabel II. (Translator's note.)

ditional sentiment of fear and reverence, which was no more firmly fixed in them than the monastery belfry on its foundations; and that each man, feeling himself violently stirred by a sudden, inexplicable impulse, hurled himself onto the corpse with a mixture of valour and horror, of fury and remorse. Without doubt monasticism covers many abuses, and fosters a great deal of egoism; religion is very deep-rooted in Spain, and doubtlessly more than one of the demolishers repented, and confessed the next day to the holy person whom he had just thrown out of his sanctuary. But in the heart of the most ignorant and blindest man there is something that makes him thrill with enthusiasm, even frenzy, when fate confers a supreme mission on him.

The Spanish people had built with their money and their sweat the pretentious mansions of the regular clergy, to whose doors they had been going for centuries to be given the groat or farthing of idle beggary and the bread of intellectual bondage. They had shared in the clergy's felonies, they had been a party to their baseness; they had lighted the pyres of the Inquisition; they had been accomplices and informers in the atrocious persecution directed against entire races that they had wanted to root out from their midst. And after consummating the ruin of the Jews who had enriched them, and expelling the Arabs to whom they owed their civilization and their greatness, they received the chastisement of misery and ignorance. They had the endurance and the piety not to rebel against that clergy which was their handiwork, their corrupter and their scourge. They suffered for a long time under this yoke, fashioned by their own hands. And then one day, bold and strange voices poured words of independence and liberty into their ears and conscience. They realised the error of their predecessors, they were ashamed of their brutalization, they felt outraged at their wretchedness, and in spite of the idolization which they still had for images and holy relics, they smashed these idols and thought more about their rights than about worship.

What then is this secret power which suddenly transformed a devout and pious person, and made him direct his former fanaticism against the very objects which had been the driving force of his religious faith all his life? It is assuredly neither man's restlessness, nor his boredom with things in general. It is his dissatisfaction with himself, and his abhorrence of his own nervous fear.

And the Spanish people showed themselves on that day to be greater than one would have thought. They accomplished a decisive action and removed the influence which might have lead them to recant, like a child who wants to become a man, and breaks his toys so as not to give way to the temptation of playing with them again.

With regard to Don Juan Mendizabal (whose name deserves to be mentioned in connection with these events), if what I have heard about his political life is really true, he must be a man of ideals rather than a man of action, and in my opinion that is the best thing one can say about him. And the fact that this public figure sometimes expected too much from the intellectual situation in Spain, and other times hesitated unduly, that he often took inopportune half-measures and sowed his ideas in sterile ground where the seed produced nothing, all this would perhaps be sufficient pretext for denying him the skill in execution and firmness of character necessary for the success of his enterprises. But this is no reason why History, considered from a philosophical point of view (which is not often the case), should not honour him one day as being one of the most generous and ardently progressive spirits in Spain.

These reflections came to me among the ruins of the monasteries in Majorca, and whenever I heard his name being cursed, and it was maybe inadvisable for us to mention it with praise and sympathy. Then I told myself that, apart from political questions of the moment (which I admit are not to my liking nor in my line), I was able to pass judgment on man and his actions in a analytical manner, without too much risk of self-deception. It is not so necessary as is generally believed and stated to know a country inside-out and to have studied thoroughly its customs and material life, in order to have a clear idea and a real understanding of its history, its future and, in a word, its moral character. I believe there is in the general history of human life a grand design to follow which is the same for all peoples, and to which the threads of their particular history are linked. This grand design consists of the longing and perpetual striving for the ideal or, if you wish, perfectibility, which man has always carried within him like a blind instinct or as a guiding principle.

Veritably outstanding men have felt this and have practised it more or less in their own way; and the most audacious, the ones who have had the most lucid revelation of it, and have fought most in the present in order to hasten the development of the future, are those who have almost always been worst judged by their contemporaries. People have slandered and condemned them without knowing them; and only when the fruit of their labour has become apparent have they been put back on the pedestal from which they had been removed by some transient disappointments and some setbacks brought about by misunderstanding.

How many famous names in our French revolution have been tardily and half-heartedly rehabilitated! And how misunderstood and misjudged have their missions and work been! In Spain, Mendizabal has been one of the most severely criticized ministers, because he showed himself to be the most courageous, perhaps the only courageous one; and he has been so harshly reproached for the act which distinguishes his short period of power, the radical destruction of the monasteries, that I cannot help extolling in these pages his bold resolution, and the intoxication with which the Spanish people adopted it and put it into practice.

At least this was feeling that suddenly filled my heart at the sight of those ruins that time had not yet blackened, and which also seemed to protest against the past, and proclaim the awakening of truth in the people. I don't think I have lost my fondness and respect for the arts; I don't feel within me instincts of vengeance and barbarity, and finally I am not among those who say that veneration of the beautiful is useless, and that monasteries should be defaced and turned

98

into factories; but a convent of the Inquisition razed by the common people is a page of History, as great, as instructive, and as stirring as any Roman aqueduct or amphitheatre.

A government department which in cold blood ordered the demolition of a church, for some reason of paltry utility or absurd economy, would be carrying out a lamentable and criminal act. But a political leader who, one decisive and perilous day, sacrifices art and science for more precious gifts — reason, justice and religious liberty, and a people who, despite their pious instincts, their love of catholic pomp, and their respect for the priesthood, have enough courage and strength to execute this decree unhesitatingly, are like the crew of a ship buffeted by a storm, who, to save themselves, hurl their belongings into the sea.

Weep then, whoever wants to, over these ruins! Almost all these monuments whose downfall we generally deplore were dungeons where the soul or body of humanity languished for centuries. Come on, you poets, who, instead of lamenting the past days of the world's infancy, will glorify in their verses, over those remains of gilded baubles and bloodstained scourges, this virile age which has known how to liberate itself! A beautiful poem by Chamisso about the château of his forefathers, destroyed in the French Revolution, ends with a thought that is as novel in poetry as it is in politics:

"Blessed are you, old mansion, over which the ploughshare now passes! And blessed too is he who causes the plough to pass over you!"

After having evoked the memory of this beautiful poem, dare I transcribe a few pages which the Dominican monastery inspired me to write? Why not, for I am sure I can crave the reader's indulgence in expounding to him a phantasy which is contrary to my amour-propre and traditional ideas? May this figment of the imagination, whatever judgment it deserves, introduce a little variety into the dry catalogue of buildings which I have just been describing!

CHAPTER IV

THE CONVENT OF THE INQUISITION

AMONG the debris of a ruined monastery two men met in the moonlight. One appeared to be in the prime of life, and the other bent down under the weight of years; nevertheless, the latter was the younger of the two. Both gave a start when they came face to face, for the night was advanced, the street was deserted, and the clock chimed dolefully and slowly in the bell-tower of the Cathedral.

The one who seemed to be older spoke first:

"Whoever you are, my man, you've nothing to fear from me; I am weak and broken. Don't expect to get anything from me either, for I'm poor and destitute."

"My friend", replied the other, "I only attack those who attack me, and like you, I am too poor to be afraid of thieves".

"Brother", answered the man with haggard features, "why then did you jump when you saw me?"

"Because I am a little superstitious, like all artists, and I took you for the ghost of one of those monks who no longer exist, and whose graves we are walking over. And you, why did you jump too when you ran into me?"

"Because I am very superstitious, like all friars, and I took you for the ghost of one of those monks who buried me alive in the tombs you're treading on."

"What are you saying? Are you perchance one of those men I have been eagerly and vainly looking for all over Spain?"

"You will not see us anywhere where there is the light of the sun; but you will however be able to find us in the shades of night. Now that your hope is fulfilled, what do you want to do to this poor friar?"

"To look at you, to question you, father, to engrave your features on my mind in order to reproduce them on canvas; to listen to your words and repeat them to my fellow-countrymen; to get to know you and absorb all the mystery, poetry and greatness that there is in the person of a holy man and in the life of the cloister."

"Where do you get, my dear traveller, the strange ideas you have formed about such things? Don't you belong to a country where the domination of the Popes has been rejected, where monks are proscribed and the cloisters suppressed?"

"There are still amongst us devout souls who love the past and have fervent imaginations, saturated with the poetry of the Middle Ages. We search for, venerate and almost worship anything that can bring us a faint fragrance of the past. Don't think, father, that we are all blind profaners. We artists hate a people that tarnishes and breaks whatever it touches. Far from approving their decrees of death and destruction, we strive in our pictures, in our poetry, in our theatre and in all our works, to give life back to ancestral traditions, and to reanimate the spirit of mysticism which that sublime child, Christian art, has engendered."

"What's that you say, my son? Is it possible that the artists in your free and flourishing country are inspired by another age than the present? They have so many new things to sing about, to paint and illustrate! Why live, as you say, bowed over the ground where their forefathers are sleeping? Why look amongst the dust of tombs for a lively, fruitful inspiration when God, in his infinite goodness, has given them such a peaceful and beautiful life?"

"I don't know, good father, in what way our life is as you picture it. We artists don't bother about politics, and social problems interest us till less. We would look in vain for poetry in what goes on around us. The arts are languishing, inspiration is stifled, bad taste is paramount, everybody is concerned only with material things, and if we hadn't the culture of the past and the ancient monuments of religious faith to fortify us we would completely lose the sacred fire that we are trying so hard to hold on to."

"But people have told me that mankind has never carried the art of good living, the marvels of science and the benefits of liberty so far as in your country. Perhaps they told me wrong?"

"If they told you, father, that at one time, thanks to our material wealth, we had achieved so much well being, and extracted from the ruins of the old society an amazing diversity of pleasures, opinions and beliefs, they have told you the truth. But if they haven't added that all these things, instead of making us happy, have debased and corrupted us, they have only told you a half-truth."

"How can such a strange phenomenon have come about? Have all the sources of happiness turned to poison on your lips, and has what makes man great and just, namely liberty and gracious living, made you small and wretched? Explain this monstrous thing to me."

"My father, am I the one to remind you that man does not live by bread alone? If we have lost faith, everything we have otherwise acquired has been of no benefit to our souls."

"Tell me then, my son, how have you lost faith when, after religious persecution had ceased in your land, you would have been able to broaden your minds and lift your eyes to the divine light? That was the moment to begin believing, for it was the moment of knowledge. And at that moment, did you doubt? What cloud passed over your heads?"

"The cloud of human weakness and wickedness. Isn't it incompatible with faith to question it, father?"

103

"It's as if you asked me, young man, whether faith is incompatible with truth. Don't you believe in anything, my son? Or rather, do you believe in falsehood?"

"Alas! I only believe in art. But isn't that sufficient to give one's soul strength, confidence and sublime joy?"

"I know nothing about it, my son, and I don't understand it. Is there any happy man left among your people? And yourself, are you invulnerable to sorrow and depression?"

"No, father. Artists are the unhappiest, the most rebellious and the most tortured of men, for every day they see the object of their veneration debased, and their efforts to uplift it are in vain."

"And why do such intelligent men let the arts perish, instead of taking action to revive them?"

"It is because they now have no faith, and without faith Art is impossible."

"But haven't you just told me that art for you is a religion? My son, either you're contradicting yourself, or I'm misunderstanding you."

"But how can we not be in contradiction with ourselves, we to whom God has entrusted a mission which the world denies us? We, against whom the present shuts the doors of glory, inspiration and life; we, who see ourselves forced to live in the past, and to interrogate the dead about the secrets of eternal beauty, the cult of which the man of today has lost and whose altars he has destroyed? Before the works of the great masters, when the hope of equalling them tempts and delights us, we feel strong and enthusiastic; but when we attempt to realise our ambitious dreams, an incredulous and incomprehensible world deflates us with the coldness of its sarcasm and disdain, and we are unable to produce anything that conforms to our ideal, and ideas wither in our hearts before they are born."

The young artist spoke with bitterness. The moon lit up his proud, sad features, and the friar, motionless, looked at him with frank but friendly surprise.

"Let us sit down here" said the latter after a moment of

silence, as he stopped near the solid balustrade of a terrace that overlooked the city, the countryside and the sea. It was in the corner of that garden of the Dominicans which in other times was full of flowers, fountains and precious marble sculptures, but was now covered with rubbish and invaded by all the weeds that grow and thrive among ruins.

The traveller, in his agitation, crumpled one of these in his hand and hurled it away at once, letting out a cry of pain. The monk smiled.

"The sting is sharp", he said, "but not dangerous. My son, the brambles which you have just carelessly touched and which have pricked you, are the symbol of those coarse, rough persons of whom you were complaining a little while ago. They invade the palaces and the monasteries, they encompass the altars and establish themselves on the remains of the ancient splendours of the world. Observe with what vigour and tenacity these weeds have filled the green garden plots where we painstakingly used to grow fine, beautiful plants of which there is not one left. In the same manner, rough and simple men, who were cast aside like useless couch-grass, have regained possession of their rights and cut down the poisonous plant that grew in the shade, and was known as the Inquisition".

"And couldn't they liquidate it without destroying also the sanctuaries of Christian art, and the works of genius?"

"The cursed plant had to be torn out by the roots, because it was vigorous and rampant. They even had to destroy the foundations of these cloisters, because its roots were hidden in them."

"But, father, what is there good or beautiful about these thorny weeds that grow in their place?"

The Monk paused for an instant and replied:

"You told me you were a painter. Will you by any chance be making a picture of these ruins?"

"Of course. But why do you ask me that?"

"Will you leave out of your painting all these large weeds that cover the debris like festoons and sway in the wind, or will you make use of them as an appropriate accessory to

105

your picture, the same as I have seen in one by Salvador Rosa?"

"They are the inseparable accompaniment to ruins, and no painter would fail to take advantage of them."

"You have then, their beauty, their significance, and therefore their utility."

"Your parable is very apt, father. Put beggars and gypsies among this wreckage, and it would become more sinister and desolate. The appearance of the picture would gain, but what would humanity gain from it?"

"Perhaps a good painting, and certainly a very good lesson. But you artists who provide this lesson don't understand what you are doing, and can only see here fallen stones and weeds shooting forth."

"You are a bit hard. From what you have said, I could well answer you by saying that you can only see in this great catastrophe a liberty regained for yourself; for I suspect, father, that this monastery was not to your liking."

"My son, have you carried your love of art and poetry to the extent of living here, blind to all unpleasantness?"

"I imagine that it would have been for me the most wonderful life in the world. Oh, how vast this convent must have been and of what a noble style! How these remains proclaim its former splendour and elegance! How pleasant it must have been to come here in the evening and breathe the gentle sea breeze and dream, with the ears caressed by the sound of the waves, when these galleries were paved in rich mosaics, when the crystalline waters murmured in the marble fountains, and a silver lamp glimmered like a pale star in the depths of the sanctuary! What profound peace and majestic quiet you must have enjoyed, when the respect and confidence of men surrounded you, and when they made the sign of the cross and lowered their voices as they passed by your mysterious porticos! Who wouldn't want to abjure all their worries, all the anxieties and ambitions of worldly life to come and shut themselves up in here, in tranquility and forgetting the entire outside world, in order to devote ten perhaps twenty years to a single picture, which one would slow-

106

ly beautify like a precious diamond, until it was placed over an altar, not so that it could be judged and criticized by some ignoramus, but so that it could be revered and acknowledged as a worthy representation of the Deity itself!"

"Stranger" said the monk in a severe tone, "your words overflow with pride and your dreams are nothing more than vanity. In this art of which you speak with so much emphasis and which you extol so highly, you see only yourself, and this isolation that appeals to you would in your eyes only be a means for your own aggrandisement. Now I understand why you believe in this egoistic art, without believing in any religion or society. But it's possible that you have not thought these things out in your mind before saying them, and perhaps you don't actually know what happened in these dens of corruption and terror. Come with me, and perhaps what I show you woll change your feelings and your ideas."

The monk led the young man, not without risk, across the mountains of wreckage and over hazardous pitfalls to the middle of the destroyed monastery. There, in the place which prisoners had occupied years ago, he made him descend carefully by the walls of a massive piece of architecture about fifteen feet thick, which the spade and pickaxe had split asunder down to its foundations. In the heart of this dreadful crypt of stone and cement there could be seen, like gaping jaws in the bowels of the earth, small cells without light or air, separated one from another by walls as thick as the solid mass of masonry which weighed down on the gloomy, forbidding vaults.

"Young man", said the friar, "these holes that you see are not wells, nor even graves; they are the dungeons of the Inquisition. For several centuries all men perished in them who, guilty or innocent before God, degraded by vice or led away by passion, inspired by genius or virtue, have dared to have different ideas from those of the Inquisition. The Dominican fathers were learned men, scholars and even artists. They possessed great libraries where the refinements of theology, in volumes bound in gold and morocco leather and edged with glittering pearls and rubies, were displayed on

107

shelves of ebony. And on the other hand, when it came to man, the living book in which God wrote his thoughts with his own hand, they interred him alive and kept him in the bowels of the earth. They had vessels of engraved silver, sparkling chalices ornamented with jewelry, magnificent pictures, and figures of the Virgin in gold and marble; and yet, again when it came to man, the chosen vessel, the chalice full of heavenly grace, the living image of God, they delivered him alive to the coldness of death and to the worms of the sepulchre. The same being who cultivated roses and daffodils with as much care as would be taken with a child, would pitilessly permit a fellow-countryman, a brother, to waste away and rot in the dampness of a tomb-like cell".

"My son, that is what the monk and the cloister are like! Brutal ferocity on the one hand, cowardly terror on the other. Egoistic intelligence or devoutness without humanity, that is the Inquisition. And although on exposing these infected caverns to the light of day the hand of the liberator found some pilasters and gilded ornaments which he smashed or defaced, is it necessary on that account to replace the flagstones of the sepulchre over the dying victims, and shed tears over the fate of their executioners because they no longer have gold or slaves?"

The artist had descended into one of the cells to examine with curiosity the walls. For an instant he tried to imagine the struggle which the human mind, buried alive, had to sustain day after day against the frightful despair of such a captivity; but hardly had he drawn this picture in his impressionable imagination, when he also was filled with anguish and terror; his limbs trembled, he became short of breath, he felt he was going to swoon, and in his anxiety to escape from this hell he shouted out, extending his arms towards the monk who had remained at the entrance.

"Father, in the name of heaven help me to get out of here!"

"Very well, my son", said the friar, stretching out his hand to him, "if that's what you feel now seeing the brilliant

108

stars above your head, imagine how I felt when I saw the sunlight again after ten years of torture!"

"You also, poor fellow!", cried the traveller, hastening his steps towards the garden. "Have you been able to put up with ten years of anticipated death without losing your reason or your life? I think if I'd stayed another moment in that cell I would have gone mad. No, I never believed the sight of a dungeon could produce such sudden, profound terror, and I never thought it possible that anyone could get used to it and survive it. I have seen the instruments of torture in Venice, I have also seen the prison cells of the ducal palace, with the cul-de-sac where the victim is struck down by an invisible hand, and the flagstone full of holes through which the blood dripped and disappeared into the waters of the canal without leaving a trace. I got the impression there of a more or less rapid killing, but life in that dungeon into which I have just descended must have been the most terrible thing I can think of. My God, to be there and not to be able to die!"

"Look at me, my son", said the monk, pointing to his bald and scrawny scalp, "I am no older than what you reveal in your virile features and serene brow, and without doubt you have taken me for an old man. It doesn't matter whether I deserved or how I bore my long agony. I am not asking for your pity; I don't need it now, because today I feel young and happy when I look at these demolished walls and empty dungeons. Neither do I wish to inspire you with horror for monks. They are free, and I too. God has been good to all of us. But, since you are an artist, it will be useful for you to have experienced one of those emotions without which no artist would understand his work.

"If now you wish to paint these ruins over which, a little while ago, you were lamenting the past, and amongst which I come every night to prostrate myself and give thanks to God for the present, your hand and your genius will perhaps be inspired by thoughts more lofty than a craven nostalgia or a vain admiration. Many monuments which have an invaluable meaning for antiquarians, possess no other merit than that of recalling the deeds which humanity sanctified by their erection, and often enough those deeds were iniquitous or futile. Seeing that you have travelled, you will probably have seen in Genoa a bridge which crosses a chasm, enormous docks, a fine, massive church, erected at great cost in a lonely district to satisfy the vanity of a patrician to whom the holy water meant nothing, and who would not kneel in God's house with the worshippers of his parish. Maybe you have also admired the Pyramids in Egypt, which are a hideous testimonial to the slavery of the nations, or those prehistoric dolmens over which human blood flowed to satisfy the insatiable thirst of barbaric gods. But the majority of you artists only see in man's works the beauty and peculiar features of their execution, without appreciating the ideas which they express. That is why your own works often lack the true colour of life, especially when, instead of portraying what circulates in the veins of suffering humanity, you coldly strive to interpret something that is dead, and which you don't understand."

"Father", replied the young man, "I understand what you mean, and I don't entirely disagree with you. But do you think that art can be inspired by such a philosophy? You explain with the reasoning of our present age what was conceived in a poetical delirium by the imaginative superstition of our fathers. If instead of smiling Grecian goddesses we laid bare the commonplace figures concealed under their voluptuous forms — if in place of the divine Madonna of the Florentines we painted, like the Dutch, a buxom chambermaid — if, in short, we turned Jesus, the Son of God, into an ingenuous philosopher of the Platonic school — then, instead of Deities we would only have men, in the same way as here, in place of a Christian temple, we have in front of our eyes a heap of stones".

"My son" answered the monk, "if the Florentines have given divine features to the Virgin, it is because they believed in her, and if the Dutch have given her common features, it is because they no longer believed in her. And today you boast of painting sacred things, you who only believe in art, that is to say, in yourselves. You will never succeed. Only attempt, therefore, to paint what is tangible and appeals to you. If I had been a painter, I would have made a beautiful picture of the day of my liberation. I would have depicted in it bold, robust men, each with hammer in one hand and torch in the other, making their way into these limbos of the Inquisition which I have just shown you, and rising from the fetid ground there would be spectres with lacklustre eyes and terrified expressions. The light of the heavens would be seen, penetrating through the crevices of the destroyed vaults to rest on their heads like an aureole".

"This would have been a marvellous subject, as appropriate in my time as the Final Judgment of Michael Angelo was in his. For these men of the people, who appear to you to be so rough and despicable in their work of destruction, seemed to me more glorious and noble than the angels in heaven; the same as this ruin, which for you is an object of sadness and distress, is for me a monument of more religious significance thant it was before its fall.

"If I was entrusted with the erection of an altar designed to hand down to future generations a memorial to the greatness and might of our own, I would wish for nothing other than this mountain of wreckage, and over it, on the consecrated stone, I would inscribe the follo٧ ٦g:

"On this altar, in the times of ignorance and cruelty, men worshippcd the God of vengeance and torture. On the day of justice and in the name of humanity, the people destroyed these bloodstained stone blocks, abominable in the eyes of the God of Mercy."

CHAPTER V

It was not really in Palma but in Barcelona, in the ruins of the House of the Inquisition, where I saw these dungeons, which were openings in walls fourteen feet thick. It is very possible that there were no prisoners in those in Palma when the people demolished them. I apologize, therefore, if I have offended Majorcan susceptibilities by the poetic licence which I have taken in the passage that I have just written.

However, as nothing is invented that isn't founded to a certain extent on truth, I must make it clear that I knew a priest in Majorca, now vicar of a parish in Palma, who told me that he had spent seven years of his life, the flower of his youth, in the prisons of the Inquisition, and that he only succeeded in getting out of them thanks to the protection of a lady who took an interest in him. He was a man in the prime of life, with bright eyes and of a happy disposition, who didn't seem to miss the regime of the Holy Office very much.

In connection with this Dominican monastery, I will quote some paragraphs by Grasset de Saint-Sauveur, who cannot be accused of partiality, seeing that he wrote in flowery eulogy of the inquisitors, with whom he became acquainted in Majorca:

"There are still to be seen in the cloister of Santo Do-

113

mingo some paintings which recall the barbarities carried out a long time ago against the Jews. Each one of the poor wretches who were burnt figure in a picture, on the lower part of which one can read his name, age, and the date he was executed.

"I have been assured that, a few years ago, the descendants of these luckless persons, who form a special sect amongst the inhabitants of Palma under the ridiculous denomination of «chuetas» (screech-owls), had vainly offered substantial sums of money for the removal of these distressing reminders. I can hardly believe it...

"Anyway, I will never forget that one day, when I was walking along the cloister of the Dominican monastery, looking sadly at these doleful paintings, a monk came up to me and pointed out to me many figures in the pictures marked with cross-bones. They are, he said to me, the portraits of those who were burnt, and whose remains were thrown to the wind.

"My blood froze and I quickly went away, with my heart overcome and my senses shocked by the incident.

"By chance there fell into my hands a report, printed in the year 1755 by order of the Inquisition, which contained the Christian names, surnames, personal details and crimes of all those tried and condemned in Majorca from the year 1645 to 1691.

"Trembling, I read this document and found in it four Majorcans, one a woman, burnt alive for Judaism; another thirty-two, condemned for the same crime, who died in the dungeons and whose bodies had been burnt; three whose ashes had been exhumed and scattered in the wind; a Dutchman accused of Lutherism; a Majorcan convicted of Mohammedanism; six Portuguese, one a woman, and seven Majorcans burnt in effigy because they had had the good fortune to escape. I counted up to two hundred and sixteen victims more, including Majorcans and foreigners, accused of heresy, Judaism or Mohammedanism, who were released from prison after having publicly retracted and returned to the bosom of the Church."

114

This horrifying catalogue ended with a decree by the Inquisition, which was no less terrible. Here is the text as given by the said Grasset:

"All the criminals listed in this report have been publicly condemned by the Holy Office as acknowledged heretics, and all their possessions have been confiscated and handed over to the Royal Treasury. They are declared to be unqualified and unfit to occupy or obtain positions or benefices, both ecclesiastical and secular, or any other public or honorary offices. They are debarred from wearing on their persons, or allow to be worn by their dependants, gold, silver, pearls, precious stones, coral, silk, pure wool, and fine cloth; also they are debarred from riding on horseback, carrying arms, and exercising or using other things which by the common laws and decrees of the kingdom, and by the instructions and practices of the Holy Office are forbidden to such disgraced individuals. The same deprivation is extended to women condemned to be burnt at the stake, to their sons and daughters, and in the case of men, even to their grandchildren on the male side. At the same time, the memory of those executed in effigy is damned to hell, and it is ordered that their bones, in order to isolate them from those of true Christians, shall be dug up and handed over to the court of justice and the secular arm to be burnt and reduced to ashes. Likewise all inscriptions and titles that there may be on their tombs, or coats of arms affixed or painted on any place, will be effaced or struck off, in such a manner that there only remains on the face of the earth the memory of their sentence and execution."

When one reads such a document, from a period so close to our own, and considers the implacable hatred which, after ten or fifteen generations of Jews converted to Christianity, still pursues this unfortunate race in Majorca, it is impossible to believe that the spirit of the Inquisition will have been so completely extinguished, as was claimed at the time of Mendizabal's decree.

I will not close this chapter nor leave the convent of the Inquisition without disclosing to my readers a rather curious discovery on the part of M. Tastu which, thirty years ago, would have made the fortune of this erudite person, if he had not put it into the hands of the "master of the world", without thought of profiting by it himself, a likelihood which is much more in keeping than the other with the character of an unprejudiced and disinterested artist.

This memorandum is too interesting for me to attempt to cut it short. Here it is as it was passed on to me, with authorization to publish it:

THE MONASTERY OF SANTO DOMINGO IN PALMA DE MALLORCA

A friend of Santo Domingo, Miguel de Fabra, was the founder of the Order of the Preaching Brotherhood in Majorca. He was a native of Old Castile, and accompanied James I on the conquest of the principal Balearic island in the year 1229. His education was considerable and varied and his piety remarkable, which gave him a very strong influence over the "Conquistador", his noble companions and even his soldiers. He used to harangue the troops, administer communion to the faithful and wage war against the unfaithful, as all the ecclesiastics at that time did. The Arabs said that only the Holy Virgin and Father Miguel had conquered them. It was also said that Aragonese soldiers prayed, after God and the Virgin, to the father, Miguel de Fabra.

The illustrious Dominican had received the habit of his Order in Toulouse from the hands of his friend Domingo. The latter sent him to Paris with two other companions to carry out an important mission, and it was he who established in Palma the first Dominican monastery with the help of a donation made to him by the procurator of the primate of Majorca, D. J. R. Torella. This took place in the year 1231.

A mosque and a small patch of ground around it was used as a foundation. The founder brothers enlarged the community during the ensuing years by means of a lucrative trade in every kind of merchandise, and with donations quite frequently received from their faithful followers. The original founder, Miguel de Fabra, went away to Valencia, which place he had helped to reconquer, and died there.

Jaime Fabra was the architect of the monastery of the Dominicans. It is not stated that he was of the same family as Father Miguel, his namesake; it is known only that he completed and handed over his plans about the year 1296, and that years later he drew those for Barcelona cathedral (1317) and many other churches in the territory of the kings of Aragon.

If one examines, as we have done, the different parts of the blasted monument, it can be seen that the convent and its church must have undergone many alterations in the course of time. Here, barely standing on its feet, is a rich portal whose style corresponds to that of the 14th century; but further on, forming part of the structure, some broken arches with heavy keystones lying on the rubbish, indicate that, besides Jaime Fabra, other architects, very inferior to him, had carried on his work.

Over these vast ruins, of which only a few ancient palm trees have remained standing, preserved at our urgent request, we have deplored, as we have already done over the ruins of the convents of Santa Catalina and San Francisco in Barcelona, the fact that this senseless destruction was brought about by stony-hearted politics.

As a matter of fact, art and history have lost nothing by the fall of the monasteries of San Jeronimo in Palma, and San Francisco in Barcelona, bordering on the *muralla de mar* (sea-wall). But in the name of history, and in the name of art, why not have preserved, as monuments, the convents of Santa Catalina in Barcelona, and Santo Domingo in Palma, whose aisles concealed the tombs of people of great note, "las sepulturas de personas de be", as it said in a small booklet we had in our hands, and which formed part of the archives of the place? In it were contained, besides the names of N. Cotoner, Grand Master of the Order of Malta, those of Dameto, Muntaner, Villalonga, La Romana, and Bonapart! This booklet, like everything in connection with the monastery, belongs now to the contractor for the work of demolition and clearing.

This man, a typical Majorcan, whom one didn't take to at first sight but who soon turned out to be an affable and reassuring person, noticing the interest we were taking in the ruins and historical records, and being besides, like all men of the people, an admirer of the great Napoleon, hastened to show us the tomb with the arms of the Bonaparts, his forefathers, as is the tradition in Majorca. This seemed to us curious enough to warrant some investigations on the subject, but as we were busy on other work, we weren't able to devote the time and attention necessary to complete them.

We found the coat of arms of the Bonaparts, which are:

A quarter of azure, with stars of six points gold, two, two, and two, a field of gules with lion of gold spotted, a chief of gold charged with a rising eagle sable.

1.   In a book on heraldry, which is one of the treasures in the Count of Montenegro's library, we obtained a facsimile of these arms.

2.   In Barcelona there is another Spanish book on heraldry, not very well produced, the property of the archivist to the Crown of Aragon. In this proofs are to be found, dated the 15th June 1549, of the nobility of the Fortuny family, among whose four quarters figures that of the maternal ancestor of the Bonapart family.

In the registry we found the "Indice: Pedro III", volume II, from the archives of the Crown of Aragon. In this mention is made of two acts, dated in the year 1276, relative to members of the "Bonpar" family. This name, of Provençal or Languedoc origin, underwent alteration in Majorca, like so many others at the same time, and was changed into "Bonapart".

In 1411, Hugo Bonapart, a native of Majorca, went to the island of Corsica in the capacity of regent or governor for King Martin of Aragon, and the origin of the Bonapartes is traced back to him. Thus, Bonapart is the Romanesque name, Bonaparte the old Italian, and Buonaparte the modern Italian. It is known that members of Napolen's family signed themselves indifferently Bonaparte or Buonaparte.

Who knows what importance these trifling details might have had if they had come to light long ago, and Napoleon, who so much wanted to be French, had been aware that his family originated in France?

Although the discovery of M. Tastu doesn't have the same political importance today, it is none the less interesting on that account; and if I had a voice in the matter of the funds granted by the French government to the learned professions, I would try to ensure that this particular biographer had the necessary means to complete his studies.

It matters very little now, I realise, that the French origin of Napoleon is confirmed. This great captain, who to my way of thinking (for which of course I beg to apologise) was not such a great prince, but who was by his personal character certainly a very great man, succeeded in having himself adopted by France, and posterity will never ask whether his antecedents were Florentine, Corsican, Majorcan, or from Languedoc. However, history will always be interested in lifting the veil on this predestined family, of which certainly Napoleon is no fortuitous accident or isolated incident. I am sure that if we searched carefully, we would find in previous generations men and women befitting such a descendant; and it is here that armorial bearings, those insignia which the law of equality has condemned, but which the historian will always make use of as providing significant data, could throw some light on the warlike or ambitious destiny of the former Bonapartes.

Actually, was there ever a coat of arms more arrogant and symbolic than that of those Majorcan knights? The lion in fighting attitude, the sky strewn with stars from which the prophetic eagle is trying to free itself, are they not something like the mysterious hieroglyphs of a most uncommon fate? And Napoleon who loved the poetry of the stars with a kind of superstition and gave the eagle to France as a heraldic device, did he by any chance have knowledge of his Majorcan lineage, and not being able to trace his family back to its supposed Provençal source, keep quiet about his Spanish ancestors? Such is the lot of great men after their death: to see the nations arguing over their cradles or their tombs.

BONAPART

(Obtained from a manuscript book on heraldry which contains the coats of arms of the leading families of Majorca, etc. The manuscript belonged to Don Juan Dameto, the Majorcan chronicler who died in 1633, and is kept in the library of the Count of Montenegro. It is a 16th century manuscript.)

Majorca, 20th September 1837
M. Tastu.

Proofs of the nobility of Pedro Fortuny, 13th June 1549.

No. 1
FORTUNY.

His father, of an ancient noble house of Majorca.
Field of silver, with five black roundels, two, two and one.

No. 2
COS.

His mother, of a noble house of Majorca.
Field of gules (red), a bear of gold, crowned with a fleur-de-lys of the same colour.

No. 3
BONAPART.

His paternal ancestor, of an ancient noble house of Majorca.

(Here the description of the escutcheon was missing. The dissimilarities result from whoever painted the heraldic device; he has not realised what he was copying; in addition it isn't accurate.)

120

GARI.

His maternal ancestor, of an ancient noble house of Majorca.

Quartered in gules (red) and azure (blue). Three silver towers, two and one, and three wavy bands of silver.

Part III

CHAPTER I

W E departed for Valldemosa on a cloudless morning about the middle of December to take possession of our Cartuja, caressed by the beautiful rays of an autumnal sun that was becoming more and more remarkable for us. After crossing the fertile plain around Establiments, we reached a deserted district, wooded in parts, dry and stony elsewhere, rather damp and cold, and everywhere broken up by craggy, hilly ground difficult to compare with anything I have seen in other places.

Nowhere else, except in some valleys of the Pyrenees, did nature appear so unrestricted as in this scrub-land of Majorca with its vast stretches, which led me with good reason to doubt the extensive cultivation that the Majorcans claim to have carried out in all the island.

However, I don't intend to reproach them because of that, for nothing could be more beautiful than this neglected terrain, which could produce whatever one wants and has everything: tortuous, sloping, windblown trees; horrible brambles, lovely flowers; carpets of grass, rushes, thorny caper bushes, fine delightful asphodels. And many other things fashioned according to God's will: a ravine, a hill, a stony path ending abruptly in a quarry; a verdant track plunging

125

down unexpectedly to a deceptive rivulet; unenclosed mea-
dow-land ending suddenly before a peak-topped mountain;
thickets strewn with large rocks that look as though they
have fallen from the sky; roads excavated along the edge of
the torrent, between bushes of myrtle and honeysuckle; and
a farmhouse, placed there like an oasis deep in the desert,
with its palm tree rising up like a look-out to guide the traveller on his lonely way.

Switzerland and the Tyrol for me have not had the same
look of free and primitive creation that I found so fascinating
in Majorca. It seemed to me that in the wildest parts of the
Helvetic mountains Nature, abandoned to the over-rough at-
mospheric conditions, only escaped the hand of man to receive intolerable chastisement from the heavens, and to suffer, like a fiery soul in torment, the bondage of its own
convulsions. Majorca, on the other hand, thrives under the
kiss of a glowing sky and smiles at the blows of the mild
squalls that pass lightly over it as they traverse the sea. The
bent over flower straightens itself and is stronger, and the
snapped off trunk sends out more vigorous shoots than ever
after the storm; and although, to be exact, there are no wild-
ernesses in the island, the lack of roads gives it an air of
desertion or absence of law, which must be something like
the magnificent savannahs of Louisiana, where, in my youth-
ful dreams, I used to follow René Chateaubriand in search
of the footsteps of Atala or Chactas.

I am sure that this eulogy of Majorca will not please the
Majorcans very much, because they claim to have very nice
roads. Nice to look at, I won't deny; but as for being practicable for vehicles, you will be able to judge for yourself.

The conveyance most used in the island is a two-wheeled
carriage called the "tartana", a kind of *coucou-omnibus* (the
hire-cab in Paris), drawn by one horse or a mule, and without springs of any sort. There is also the *birlocho,* a sort of
light four-seat coach, designed on the same lines as the "tartana", and fitted like the latter with solid-rimmed wheels,
massive ironwork, and upholstered in the interior with flock
wool. I may say that you can't help feeling a little suspicious

when getting into this vehicle with such a comfortable appearance, for the first time!

The coachman sits on a small plank which acts as the driving seat, with his feet apart and resting on the shafts, and with the rump of the horse between his legs; so that he has the advantage of not only feeling all the bumps of the wagonette, but also all the violent movements of the animal, as if he was riding the horse and the carriage at the same time. However he doesn't appear to be unhappy to travel like this, for he sings continuously no matter how terrible the shocks he suffers, and only stops to utter, quite phlegmatically, some forthright oaths when his horse hesitates going down some steep slope or negotiating a hilly stretch of the route.

And that is how one journeys; ravines, torrents, quickset and ditches, all present no difficulty. You don't stop for such trifling things. Besides, it is supposed to be the road.

On setting off, you take this obstacle race as a wager in rather bad taste, and you ask the driver what his game is.

"It's the road" he tells you.

"But, this torrent?"

"It's the road."

"And this deep hole?"

"It's the road."

"And this bush also?"

"It's still the road."

"Oh, very well!"

After that there is nothing better to do than resign yourself to it, to bless the quilting that covers the body of the carriage, and without which you would assuredly emerge with broken bones; to confide your soul to God and contemplate the scenery, awaiting either death or a miracle.

And yet you sometimes arrive safe and sound, thanks to the steadiness of the vehicle, to the strong legs of the horse, and perhaps to the careless indifference of the coachman, who lets the animal have its head, folds his arms, and quietly smokes his cigar whilst one wheel runs along the edge of the hillside or in the ditch.

127

People soon become used to danger when they see the rest taking no notice of it, although it may be very real. The carriage doesn't overturn every day; but when it does it's difficult to avoid getting hurt. The year before our arrival, Tastu had suffered an accident of this kind on the same road from Establiments that we took, and was given up on the spot for dead. He had a legacy of some horrible head-aches to remind him of it, but they didn't dampen his desire to go back to Majorca.

Almost all the country people have a vehicle of some sort, and the nobility still have large coaches of the time of Louis XIV, with wide bodies, some with eight windows, and whose enormous wheels defy every obstacle. Four or six strong mules swiftly pull these heavy, badly suspended conveyances. They are grotesquely ungainly, but spacious and solid, in which you cross at full speed and with incredible audacity the most terrible defiles, but not without finishing the journey with a few bruises, knocks on the head, or at least with some aching joints.

The serious Miguel de Vargas, a truly Spanish author who never jokes, speaks in the following terms of the *horrorosos caminos* (frigthful roads) in Majorca:

"In a certain important respect it is impossible to exaggerate the pitiful condition of this Balearic island. What they call a road is a chain of impassable chasms, and the journey from Palma to the mountains of Galatzo offers the unfortunate passenger death at every step."

On the outskirts of the towns and villages the roads are not so dangerous, but they have the serious disadvantage of being enclosed between two walls or side-ditches, which doesn't allow the passage of two vehicles. When this happens, it is necessary to unyoke the bullocks from the wagon, or unhook the horses from the carriage, so that one of the two can go back, generally for a long distance. Then a long argument breaks out about which one of them must move backwards; and during this time the delayed traveller can do nothing better than repeat to himself the Majorcan motto *mucha calma,* for his own particular edification.

128

The Cartuja, according to a lithograph by J. B. Laurens, which illustrates his «Souvenirs d'un voyage d'art a l'ile de Majorque, 1840».

George Sand and her family went up this stony slope to get to their lodgings in the Cartuja of Valldemosa, in 1838. (Lithograph by Laurens)

Apart from the little that the upkeep of their roads costs them, the Majorcans have another advantage: they have a choice of several routes, and the only difficulty is to select the right one. I have been three times from the Cartuja to Palma only, and vice versa. Six times I went by a different road, and each time the *birlocho* lost the way, causing us to wander over hills and through valleys with the driver making the pretext that he was looking for a seventh route, which he said was better than the others, but he never could find it.

It is three leagues from Palma to Valldemosa, but three Majorcan leagues, which can't be covered driving fast in under three hours. The road rises imperceptibly for the first two. During the third it enters the mountains and leads up a well paved slope (possibly a former work of the Carthusian monks), but very narrow, horribly steep, and more dangerous than the rest of the way.

There one has one's first chance to admire the Alpine part of Majorca. But it is not enough that the mountains rise up on either side of the gorge, and that the torrent leaps from rock to rock; only in the heart of winter do these regions take on the wild, untamed aspect that the Majorcans attribute to them. In the month of December, and in spite of recent rains, the torrent was still a delightful stream which glided along among tufts of grass and clusters of flowers; the mountain was in a smiling mood, and the valley in which Valldemosa nestled opened before us like a garden in Spring.

To reach the Cartuja you have to leave the coach, for it is impossible for any vehicle to clamber up the stony track that leads to it. It is a fascinating approach with its sudden twists and bends among magnificent trees, and with wonderful views that are unfolded at every step, and increase in beauty the higher one rises. I have seen nothing more pleasing nor at the same time more melancholy than these prospects where the green holm oak, the carob tree, the pine, the olive, the poplar and the cypress mix their various hues in

129

9

dense masses of foliage, veritable abysses of verdure amongst which the torrent pursues its course through thickets of gorgeous richness and inimitable attraction. I will never forget a certain bend in the defile from where, turning round, one can see high up on a mountain one of those pretty Arabic type cottages which I have already described, half hidden among the leaves of the prickly pears, and, projecting its silhouette into the air, a great palm tree leaning over the chasm. When the mud and fog of Paris overwhelm me with depression, I shut my eyes and see again, as in a dream, that mountain full of greenery, those bare rocks, and that solitary palm, alone in a rose-coloured sky.

The Valldemosa cordillera rises up in a series of plateaux, becoming narrower and narrower until they form a kind of funnel, surrounded by high mountains and shut in on the north by the slope of the last plateau, at the entrance to which stands the monastery.

The Carthusian monks, through the work of years, have modified the ruggedness of this romantic spot. At the head of the valley where it reaches the hillside, they have made a vast garden, surrounded by walls that do not block the view, and to which a belt of cypress trees, in pyramidal form and disposed irregularly in pairs, give an appearance appropriate to a stage-set graveyard.

This garden, with palm and almond trees, occupies the whole inclined background of the valley, and rises in a succession of wide terraces on the lower slopes of the mountain. By moonlight, and when its irregularity is masked by the darkness, it could be taken for an amphitheatre carved out for the battles of giants. In the centre and under a group of lovely palms, a stone-built reservoir collects the water from the mountain springs, and distributes it to the lower terraces by means of paved channels, similar to those which irrigate the environs of Barcelona. These works are on too great a scale and too ingenious not to have been the creation of the Moors. They are spread over the whole interior of the island, and the channels that start at the garden of the Carthusian monks, skirt the bed of the torrent and take running water to Palma at all seasons.[1]

The Cartuja, situated at the highest point of this gorge, looks on the north side over an extensive valley which widens out and rises in a gentle slope to the coastal cliffs, whose base is battered and eroded by the sea. One arm of the cordillera points towards Spain, and the others towards the Orient. From this picturesque Carthusian monastery therefore, the sea can be glimpsed or sensed on two sides. Whilst its roar is audible to the north, it can be descried to the south like a fine, brilliant line beyond the descending mountain slopes and the immense plain which is revealed to the eye. It is a surpassing picture, framed in the foreground by dark, pine-covered crags; beyond that by the sharply outlined profiles of mountains set off by superb trees; and in the background by the rounded humps of hills, which the setting sun gilds with the warmest shades, and on whose crests one can still distinguish, from a distance of a league, the microscopic outlines of the trees, as fine as the antennae of butterflies, as black and distinct as a trace of Chinese ink on a backdrop of sparkling gold.

The luminescent centre-piece is the plain, and at that distance, when the mist from the mountains begins to form and throw a veil over the expanse of land, one could believe that it really was the sea. But the sea is much further off yet, and when the sun reappears and the plain is like a blue lake, the Mediterranean traces a band of vivid silver on the confines of this dazzling vista.

This is one of those panoramas that calm the spirit, because there is nothing left for us to desire or imagine. Everything that the painter or the poet can dream of has been created by nature in this place: a tremendous general effect, infinite detail, inexhaustible variety, confused shapes, defi-

1. All this is pure fantasy on the part of the authoress. No such canalization extended to the interior of the island; neither did water from the Cartuja ever reach Palma, whose sources of natural water supply were already in the times of the authores much nearer to the city. (*Translator's note.*)

nite outlines, vague depths, they are all there, and art can add nothing more. A man's inner sense is not always sufficient to enable him to appreciate and understand God's work; and when he thinks things over deeply, he realises his incapacity to portray in any way at all that boundlessness of life which both enslaves him and enthralls him. I would advise all persons who are consumed by the vanity of art to go and look at these landscapes, and to look at them often. I believe they would acquire the respect they are lacking for that divine art that presides over the eternal creation of things, of at least so I imagine.

In regard to myself, I have never felt more the uselessness of words than during those hours of observation I passed in the Cartuja. I was often beset by fits of religious fervour, but I could think of no better expression of exaltation than to say, "Oh God, blessed art thou for having given me such good eyes!"

Furthermore, I think that if the accidental enjoyment of such a sublime spectacle is salutary and refreshing, to have it with you always would be dangerous. One gets used to living under the influence of stirring emotions, and the factor contributing to their abuse is boredom or familiarity. Thus can be explained the incuriosity of monks in general towards the poetry of their monasteries, and the indifference of shepherds and country people towards the beauty of their mountains.

We didn't have time to get tired of all this, for the mist descended practically every evening at sunset, and hastened the close of the day, which was already short enough in that mountain retreat. Up to midday we were enveloped in the shadow of the great mountain to our left, and at three o'clock in the afternoon we fell again into the shade of the eminence on our right. But, what beautiful lighting effects we could study when the oblique rays, penetrating the breaks in the crags or skimming the summits, traced splashes of gold in the middle distance!

Sometimes our cypress trees, black obelisks which acted as a foreground to the picture, had their tops bathed in this rainbow-hued radiance. The bunches of dates on the palm trees looked like clusters or rubies, and a long dark line cut the valley obliquely and divided it into two zones, one full of the splendours of summer, the other bluish and cold to the eye, like a scene in winter.

In accordance with the Carthusian rule, thirteen monks, including the superior, lived in the Cartuja in Valldemosa. It had escaped the decree which in 1836 ordered the demolition of monasteries occupied by less than a dozen persons conjointly; but, like all the others, they had been dispersed and the convent suppressed, to be considered, as it were, the property of the State. The Majorcan government, not knowing what to do with these immense buildings, had decided to let the cells to persons who would care to occupy them, in the expectation that time and negligence would cause the place to decay and fall down. In spite of the rents being extremely moderate, the villagers in Valldemosa had not chosen to take advantage of the offer, possibly because of their extreme piety and the affection they had felt for the monks, and perhaps also through superstitious fear; this did not prevent them going there to dance on carnival nights, although they did not cease to look very much askance at our irreverent presence among those venerable walls.

Nevertheless, the Cartuja was inhabited during the summer months by middle-class people from Palma who, at that altitude and under the monastery's thick arches, undoubtedly found the air fresher than on the plain or in the city. But with the approach of winter, the cold drove them away, and when we lived in it the Cartuja had as its only inhabitants, besides myself and my family, the apothecary, the sacristan, and Maria Antonia.

Maria Antonia was a kind of housekeeper who had come from the mainland I believe to get away from squalor and poverty, and she had rented a cell in order to exploit the transient occupants of the Cartuja. Her cell was located next to ours and we made use of it as a kitchen, while she declared herself to be our factotum and help. She had been good-looking and was elegant, clean in appearance and pleasant.

133

She said she came from a good family, had delightful manners, a nice voice, and an ingratiating demeanour. She exercised a very curious sort of hospitality; she would offer her services to the new arrivals and refuse, with an offended air and almost turning pale at the idea, any kind of recompense for her attentions. She did it, she asserted, for the love of God, to be of assistance, and with the sole object of winning the friendship of her neighbours. Her entire furniture consisted of a small folding bed, a foot-warmer, two wicker chairs, a crucifix, and some earthenware crockery, all of which she put at our disposal with great generosity, allowing us to accomodate our new servant, and store our pots and pans, in her dwelling.

But she would immediately take charge of all your belongings, and reserve for herself the best of your finery and food. I have never seen a godly person so fond of her stomach, nor fingers so quick to dip down into a boiling pot without getting burnt, nor a throstle so supple to swallow the coffee and sugar of her dear lodgers, stealthily, whilst she hummed a popular air or a bolero. It would have been interesting and amusing, if one had been completely disinterested in the matter, to see the good Antonia, Catalina the queer witch-like Valldemosa woman who was our maid, and the *nina* (little girl), a small dishevelled monstrosity who acted as our errand girl, quarrelling among themselves over our food. It was the hour of the Angelus and the three never failed to recite it. The two elders, praying in unison, put their hands into every dish, and the small one, as she answered *Amen,* succeeded in palming some chop or candied fruit with unequalled dexterity. It was quite something to watch and worth while pretending not to notice; but when the rains cut communication with Palma and our provisions diminished, the "assistance" of Maria Antonia and her party became less pleasing; and my children and I found ourselves in the role of sentinel and relieving each other, in order to keep a watch on our food stores. I remember once hiding under the head-board of my bed a few packets of biscuits which were earmarked for breakfast the next day; and on another occasion, I had to keep a vulture's eye on some plates of fish in our cooking-stove, so as to scare away those birds of prey, who would have left us only the bones.

The sacristan was a lusty young fellow who had possibly served at mass with the Carthusian monks since his childhood; he was now the keeper of the keys of the monastery. There was a scandalous story about him. He was once convicted of and confessed to having seduced a *señorita* who had stayed some months in the Cartuja with her parents. He excused himself on the grounds that the State had only entrusted him with the guardianship of the virgins in the pictures. He was not a good type by any standard, but he put on very pretentious airs. Instead of the semi-Arabic attire used by people of his class, he wore European trousers with braces, which certainly dazzled the girls of the district. His sister was the most beautiful Majorcan girl that I've seen. They didn't live in the monastery. They were rich and proud and had a house in the village; but they made a daily round of the Cartuja and were often in Maria Antonia's cell, who invited them to partake of our provender when she had no appetite herself.

The apothecary was a Carthusian who used to shut himself in his cell, put on his former white robe, and recite his office all alone. As soon as anyone knocked on his door to ask him for some marsh-mallow or couch-grass root (the only specific remedies he possessed), he would quickly hide his habit under his bed and appear in black breeches, stockings and a short pea-jacket, the same as worn by the male ballet dancers in Molière's interludes. He was a very mistrustful person who never ceased complaining, and who perhaps prayed for the triumph of Don Carlos and the return of the Holy Inquisition, but he meant no harm to anybody. He sold us his herbs at the price of gold, and consoled himself with these small gains, having been released from his vow of poverty. His cell was a fairly long way from ours, being situated at the entrance to the monastery in a hidden corner, whose door was camouflaged by castor-oil bushes and other medicinal plants of pleasing aspect. Shut up there, like an

135

old hare frightened of having the dogs put on his track, he was rarely to be seen, and if we hadn't gone to him for some of his sedatives, we would never have guessed that a Carthusian monk was still living in the Cartuja.

The Cartuja has no particular architectural beauty, but is an assemblage of very solidly built roomy buildings. An army corps could be housed in a similar enclosure constructed of such a mass of stone blocks, and yet this large edifice had been erected to house twelve persons. There are twelve cells in the new cloister (for this monastery is composed of three cartujas joined together at different times), each cell consisting of three spacious rooms, which lead off one side of the cloister. Twelve chapels are located on the two sides of the building, for each monk had his own in which he used to closet himself to pray alone. All these chapels are differently decorated, covered in moldings and paintings in the crudest taste, and have painted wooden statues of saints so horrible that I confess that I would not like to meet them out of their niches at night-time. The floors of these oratories are of enamelled tiles, arranged in various mosaic designs, giving a very striking effect. In this, the Arab style still prevails, and it is the only piece of good taste that has been handed down during the centuries in Majorca. Finally, each one of these cells is provided with a cistern or trough, made out of the beautiful marble of the country, with water from which every monk was obliged to clean his chapel daily. In these vaulted and shaded places there is such a cool atmosphere that he could well have extracted a sort of luxury out of the long hours devoted to praying during the hot dog-days of summer.

Leading off the other side of the new cloister there is a fine church, whose freshness and cleanliness contrast with the air of desertion and solitude of the monastery. Close by near the centre of the cloister there is a small courtyard, symmetrically planted with box-trees which have not yet completely lost the pyramidal shape given to them by the shears of the monks. We hoped to find an organ in the church, but we forgot the rule of the Carthusians that does away with any musical instrument as being a vain luxury and a sensual pleasure. There is one single nave, paved with beautiful glazed tiles, very finely painted in floral designs, artistically arranged as on a carpet. The panelled ceiling of carved wood, the confessionals and the doors are of extreme simplicity; but the perfection of the moldings, and the impeccability and delicacy of the ornamental work, testify to a skill in workmanship that is not generally found any longer in cabinetwork in France. Unfortunately, this highly specialised craft has been lost also in Majorca. In the whole island, M. Tastu has told me, there are only two artisans who have kept up this artistic profession. The carpenter we employed at the Cartuja was certainly an artist, but only in regard to music and painting. When he came one day to our cell to put up some white wooden shelves, he looked at all our scanty artist's equipment with that curiosity that hovers between the ingenuous and the indiscreet, which I had noticed before among Slavonic Greeks. The sketches which my son had done, inspired by Goya's pictures, depicting monks having a party, and with which he had decorated the walls of our room rather shocked him; but when he discovered the Descent from the Cross, an engraving from Ruben's painting, he stood for a long time absorbed in strange contemplation. We asked him how he liked it, and he replied in his patois: "In the whole of Majorca there is nothing so beautiful or so natural".

This word *natural,* from the lips of a peasant who had the wild head of hair and manners of a savage, impressed us very much. The sound of the piano and the work of the painter threw him into a kind of rapture. He would leave his job and come and place himself behind the executant's chair, with mouth open and goggle-eyed. These lofty tastes or instincts didn't prevent him being as dishonest as the rest of the country people with foreigners, without any scruple whatever, although they observe a religious loyalty in their own mutual relationships. He asked a fabulous price for his work, and could hardly keep his hands off the small utensils of French manufacture which we had brought with us for our use. I had a lot of trouble in preventing articles from my dressing-table falling into his ample pockets. What tempted him most was a cut-glass tumbler, or perhaps the tooth-brush that was in it, and whose purpose he certainly didn't understand. This man had the artistic feelings of an Italian, and the predatory instincts of a Malay or a Kaffir.

In this digression I must not fail to mention the only artistic piece that we came across in the Cartuja. It was a statue of Saint Bruno in painted wood, placed in the church. The sculpture and colouring were remarkable; the admirably studied hands were held in an attitude of pious and heart-rending supplication, and the expression on the face was truly sublime in its faith and anguish. And yet it was the work of an ignorant person, for the statue standing opposite and executed by the same artist, was very poor in every concept. But when he created St. Bruno, he had undoubtedly had a stroke of inspiration, a breath of religious exaltation, which had raised him above himself. I doubt whether the saint of Grenoble has been understood and represented at any other time with such profound feeling; it was the personification of Christian asceticism.

The old cloister, which you have to go through to get into the new one, communicates with it via a quite simple deviation, but which, due to my bad sense of locality, I could never find without losing myself primarily in the third cloister.

The latter, which should be called the first cloister as it is the oldest, is also the smallest. It presents a delightful aspect. The courtyard enclosed by its cracked walls was the former cemetery of the monks. No inscriptions distinguish the graves which the friars dug themselves in their lifetime, for all memory of them was supposed to be lost in the nothingness of death. The graves could just about be detected by the slight swellings of the turf. Laurens has reproduced the physiognomy of this cloister in a delightful drawing in which I saw again with unbelievable joy the small well with its low, pointed roof, the windows with stone trellis-work from which hang down in festoons all the creeping plants and weeds associated with ruins, and the vertical cypress trees which rise up in the night like black spectres around the white wooden cross. I am sorry Laurens hasn't seen the moon rise behind the beautiful amber coloured mountain which overlooks this cloister, and that he didn't put in the foreground of his sketch an old laurel tree with an enormous trunk and withered top, which perhaps no longer existed when he visited the Cartuja. But I did find in his drawing, and specially mentioned in his writing, the beautiful dwarf palm (chamaerops), that I had to protect against the naturalistic zeal of my children, and which is possibly one of the sturdiest examples in Europe of its kind.

Around this small cloister are grouped the old chapels of the 15th century. They are always hermetically sealed, and the sacristan will open them for nobody, a circumstance that greatly excited our curiosity. By dint of looking through the crevices, we thought we could make out the remains of beautiful furniture and some very ancient carved work. Perhaps in these mysterious chambers there could be a lot of wealth shut up, from which no one in Majorca will bother to wipe the dust.

The second cloister has twelve cells and twelve chapels, like the others. Its arches, in spite of their ruinous state, have a great deal of character. They are standing up by a miracle and when we went through them one evening as a strong wind was blowing off the sea, we commended our souls to God; for no hurricane lashes the Cartuja without causing a piece of wall or a fragment of arch to fall. Never had I heard the wind wail and resound with such force, nor howl so desperately as in these crumbling and re-echoing ruins. The noise of the torrents, the racing clouds, the immense and monotonous clamour of the sea interrupted by the whistling of the wind, the terror-stricken outcries of the sea-birds caught in the violent gusts — then a thick mist which fell suddenly like a curtain, infiltrating along the cloisters under the cracked archways, making us invisible and turning the small lamp we carried to guide us into a will-o'-the-wisp floating along the galleries, and a thousand other details of that monastery life crowd en masse into my memory. For us, all this turned the Cartuja into the most romantic place in the world.

I felt happy to be able to see in its fullness and reality what I had only seen in my dreams, or in classical ballads, or in the nuns' act in Robert the Devil, at the opera. Neither did we lack fantastic apparitions, as I shall tell you later. And the influence of all this romanticism which was revealed to me there, started me reflecting on romanticism in general.

To the many parts of the edifice I have described must be added that set aside for the Father Superior, which, together with some other hidden corners, we were unable to visit, such as: the cells of the lay-brothers, a small church belonging to the old Cartuja, many places reserved for persons of quality who went there to go into retreat or fulfil religious penances, some small patios surrounded by cattle-sheds for the community's animals, rooms for the long succession of visitors, and finally, a spacious social centre, as we would say today, under the benediction of the Virgin and St. Bruno.

When the weather was very bad and prevented us roaming round the mountain, we went for our walk under the roof of the convent, and so we had plenty of time to explore the huge building. I don't know what the strange attraction was that urged me on to wrest from those deserted walls the intimate secret of the monastic life. Its traces were so recent that it seemed I could always hear the light steps of the sandals on the paving-stones, and the murmur of prayers under the arched ceilings of the chapels. In our cells, legible Latin orisons could still be seen, printed and stuck to the walls, and even in obscure hiding-places where I would never have imagined anyone saying an *oremus*.

One day when we were walking by chance through the upper corridors, we discovered a pleasing arched recess from where we could look down into a sizeable and beautiful chapel, so well furnished and in such good order that it seemed to have been abandoned only the day before. The large chair of the father superior was still in its place, and the order of religious exercises for the week, posted up in a black wood frame, was hanging on the arch in the middle of the choir stalls.

Each stall had the image of a saint fixed to the back, probably the patron saint of each monk. The smell of incense had impregnated the walls for so long that it had not yet completely dissipated. The altars were decorated with withered flowers, and the long wax tapers, half consumed, still stood erect in their brackets. The orderliness and state of preservation of these objects contrasted with the ruins of the outside, with the creeping brambles which had already reached the windows, and with the voices of the urchins who were playing quoits in the cloisters with pieces of old mosaic.

As to my children, their love for the miraculous incited them even more than us to undertake these lively, exciting voyages of exploration. My daughter was confident she would come across some fairy palace full of marvellous things in the attics of the Cartuja; and my son hoped to find the evidence of some terrible and extraordinary drama hidden among the ruins. Frequently I was scared seeing them crawling like cats along sagging beams and shaky terraces; and every time they went ahead of me and disappeared up one of the spiral stairways, I thought I'd lost them for ever, and hastened my steps with a kind of fear mixed, for some obscure reason, with superstition.

For it was useless trying to deny it; those sinister abodes, consecrated to a creed which we suspected to be sinister also, acted on our imaginations, and I would defy the coolest and calmest brain to remain perfectly normal there for long. These minor fantastic fears, if I may so call them, do not lack a certain allurement, but it is necessary to combat them in our innermost being. I confess that I have never gone along the cloister at night without feeling a queer mixture of uneasiness and pleasure, which I took care not to let my children see in case I should cause them to share it with me. And yet they didn't seem to be affected at all, for they used to run gaily in the moonlight under the broken arches which, in reality, gave the impression of being more the place for

141

convening a witches' Sabbath. Many times have I taken them to the cemetery[2] around midnight.

However, I didn't let them go out alone at night-time after we once met a very tall, old man walking in the darkness. He was a former servant or hanger-on of the brotherhood, who spent his time between wine and worship. When he was drunk he liked to wander round the cloisters, knock on the doors of the deserted cells with his pilgrim's staff, call on the monks with tipsy abuse, and pray in front of the chapels in a mournful voice. As soon as he saw a chink of light escaping from our cell, he came up to it uttering threats and swearing dreadfully. He would go into Maria Antonia's abode, who was frightened of him, and preach long sermons to her interspersed with cynical oaths, and install himself next to her brazier as if he owned the place, until the sacristan came and enticed him away with soft words and subtle inducements; for the sacristan wasn't a very brave person, and he was afraid of making an enemy. Then he used to knock on our door at unseasonable hours, and when he grew tired of calling in vain on Father Nicholas, who was his obsession, he would subside at the feet of the Virgin, whose niche was situated a few steps from our door, and sleep with an open knife in one hand, and a rosary in the other.

His disturbances didn't worry us much because he wasn't the sort to make sudden attacks on people, and as he announced his approach from afar with his inarticulate ejaculations, and by the noise of his staff on the flagstones, there was time to beat a retreat before this wild animal. The double oak door of our cell could have withstood a much more formidable siege, but the reiterated assault on nights when we had a prostrate sick person, who was thereby deprived of hours of rest, wasn't always funny. We had to put up with it with *mucha calma,* for, of course, it would have been useless to ask for help from the local police. We didn't go to mass, and our enemy was a holy man who never missed.

2. This refers to the graveyard of the Carthusian monks. (*Translator's note.*)

One night we had an alarm and apparition of another kind which I shall never forget. At first it was an unexplainable noise, which I could only compare with that of thousands of bags of nuts being rolled continuously on a pavement. We went out hurriedly into the cloister to see what was happening. It was deserted and dark as usual, but the noise was getting steadily nearer. Soon a weak glow illuminated the vast depth of the vaulted corridor, which gradually became filled with light from the glare of a large number of torches; and we saw appearing in the red fumes a great crowd of beings abominable to God and man. It was nothing less than Lucifer in person, accompanied by his whole court, a male demon, completely black, horned, with his face the colour of blood, and around him a swarm of imps with heads of birds and tails of horses and covered in tinsel of every colour, together with she-devils or shepherdesses in pink or white dresses, who gave you the impression of having been carried off by the ugly gnomes. After what I had just seen, I can assure you that for one or two minutes, and even for some time after I realised what it was all about, I had to make an enormous effort of will to keep my lamp held up to the level of the faces of that horrible throng, to which the hour, the place and the glow of the torches gave a supernatural appearance.

They were people from the village, rich farmers and middle-class persons who were celebrating Shrove Tuesday, and had come to hold a country dance in Maria Antonia's cell. The queer noise which accompanied their progress was that of the castanets, which a lot of youngsters wearing, dirty, loathsome, masks, were playing in unison, and not with the staccato, measured rhythm as in Spain, but with a continuous roll similar to drums on a battle-field. This noise, which accompanies their dances, is so persistent and trying, that one needs to have courage to endure it for a quarter of an hour. When the party has begun they interrupt it suddenly to sing a *coplita* (little ballad) in a musical style that goes on repeating itself, and makes you feel it will never end. Then the castanets renew their rolling, which lasts for three or four minutes. There is nothing more unrefined than this manner of enjoying one's self, and the resonant clicking of the wood almost bursts the ear-drums. The affected style of singing, which has no great inherent merit, achieves considerable effect when delivered thus after long intervals, by voices that have their own special quality. They are subdued in moments of maximum emphasis, and leisurely when the animation is greatest.

I imagine that the Moors sang in this way, and Monsieur Tastu, who has carried out investigations on the subject, is convinced that the popular Majorcan songs, their favourite flourishes on the guitar and manner of singing are, in a word, typically and traditionally Arabic.[3]

As soon as all these demons reached us, they surrounded us with great cordiality, for the Majorcans in general are not at all rude or hostile in their manners. King Beelzebub condescended to address me in Spanish, and told me that he was a lawyer. Then, doubtless in order to impress me still further, he tried to speak to me in French, wishing to know if I liked the Cartuja; he translated the Spanish word "cartuxa"[4] by the French word *cartouche* (cartridge), which of course was just a mistranslation; but then not even the devil in Majorca is obliged to speak all languages.

Their dancing is no gayer than their singing. We followed them to Maria Antonia's cell, which was decorated with

3. When we were going from Barcelona, on a dark and warm night, illuminated only by an extraordinary phosphorescence in the ship, most people on board were sleeping except the helsman who, to avoid the danger of doing the same, sang in a low, gentle voice as though he was afraid of waking the crew, or as if he was half asleep himself. We didn't tire of listening to him, for his singing was very attractive. He followed a rhythm with modulations quite strange to us, and it seemed he was letting his voice roam at random, like the smoke of the ship, carried away and blown about by the breeze. Some of his songs were dreamlike, a kind of idle wandering of the voice, without any particular theme but which followed the rolling of the ship and soothing murmur of the wash; and at the same time it sounded like a vague improvisation, delivered in a monotonous but pleasing style. His meditative voice overflowed with fascination. (*Author's note.*)

4. The authoress is confusing this word with the Majorcan *cartoixa.* (*Translator's note.*)

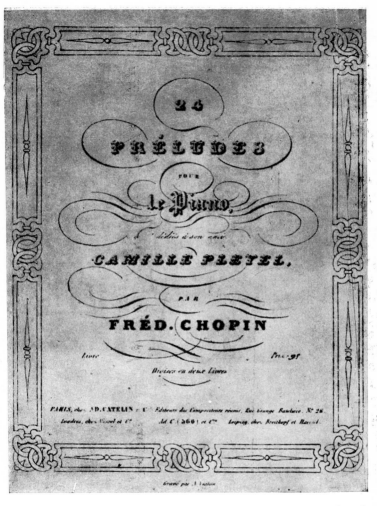

The frontispiece of the first edition of the «Preludes», composed or finised in Majorca.

First edition of the famous Third Scherzo, composed in the Cartuja
of Valldemosa,

small lanterns, and with garlands of ivy suspended across the room. Their orchestra, which consisted of one big guitar and a small one, a kind of high-pitched violin and three or four pairs of castanets, began to play *jotas* (Aragonese dances) and native *fandangos,* which were like those of the Spanish mainland but with a more original rhythm and a still more daring whirl.

The festivities were in honour of Don Rafael Torres, a rich land-holder of the district, who had married a very beautiful girl a few days earlier. The bridegroom was the only man who was supposed to dance the whole evening and with every woman, which he did, inviting one after the other. During this duet the rest of the company, grave and silent, squatted on the floor in the manner of Orientals and Africans, including the mayor in his monk's cape and with his large, silver-hilted staff.

The Majorcan bolero dancers have a hereditary gravity and none of the worldly brightness and gracefulness which are so admired in Andalusia. Men and women dance with arms extended and motionless, whilst their fingers crack the castanets smartly and continuously. The handsome Rafael danced to satisfy his conscience; and when he had exhausted his energy he went and squatted down like the others, and the young bloods took the floor and showed off in their turn. A youth, as thin as a wasp, caused general admiration by the rigidity of his movements and his leaps and bounds, which looked like galvanic springs, without his face lighting up with the slightest expression of gaiety. An enormous farm labourer, very conceited and cross-grained, tried to stretch out his leg and put his arms akimbo in the real Spanish manner; but he was ridiculed, and well he deserved it, for he was the most comical caricature imaginable. This country dance would have fascinated us for a long time if it hadn't been for the odour of rancid oil and garlic which these ladies and gentlemen exhaled, and which asphyxiated us.

The carnival disguises had less interest for us than the native costumes, which are very elegant and graceful. The women wear a kind of white coif of lace or muslin, called a

145

"rebozillo". It consists of two pieces superimposed, one of which is fastened to the head a little towards the back, and passes under the chin like a nun's veil; it is called a *rebozillo en amunt*.[5] The other piece floats like a pilgrim's cape on the shoulders, and is called the *rebozillo en volant*. The hair is parted on the forehead in two smooth tresses, which are united behind the head in a thick plait; this emerges from under the rebozillo, rests on the back and is raised to one side and supported at the waist-band. When they are in working clothes, their unplaited hair hangs flowing and loose down their backs.

The bodice is of merino wool or black silk, with short sleeves, and is tastefully adorned below the elbow and on the seams at the back with sets of metal buttons carried on silver chains. They have fine, graceful waist-lines, and very small feet which are elegantly shod on festival days. A simple country woman has lace stockings, satin shoes, a gold necklace, and several lengths of silver chains around the waist hanging from the belt. I have seen country women with very good figures, but few that were good-looking; their features were regular like those of Andalusian women, but their expression was more open and gentler. The women of the town of Soller, which I was unable to visit, have a great reputation for their beauty.

The men that I saw were not handsome, although they all appeared to be so at first sight on account of the becoming clothes they wore. The Sunday suit consists of a multi-coloured silk waistcoat, heart-shaped in cut, and very open over the chest, as is the black jacket which is short and narrow-waisted, like a woman's bodice. An immaculate white shirt, embroidered at the collar and cuffs, displays a front of the finest linen, which gives a magnificent effect to the whole turnout. They have a tight-fitting coloured sash round the waist, and wear long, baggy, striped breeches like those of the Turks, made of a silk and cotton mixture produced in the

5. A Frenchified version of the Catalan word *amunt*, meaning above, up, upwards etc. *(Translator's note.)*

146

country. With this dress go stockings of white, black, or tawny yarn, and shoes of undressed and unstained calf leather.

In their houses they put on their heads a silk or muslin scarf in the form of a turban, which suits them much better. In winter they often wear a black, woollen skullcap over their tonsure, for like the priests, these people shave the crown of the head, either for the sake of cleanliness (although, God knows, that would serve little purpose!), or as a sign of devoutness. Their thick, course, curly hair hangs about the neck in much the same way as a horse's mane. A fringe taken across the forehead with scissors completes this hairdo, cut in the style of the Middle Ages, and gives an air of energy to the face.

Their field attire, not so elaborate, is still more picturesque. According to the season, their legs are bare or encased in yellow leather leggins below the knees. When it is hot they only wear a shirt and their baggy breeches. In winter they put on a grey cape, which looks just like a monk's habit, or a large African goatskin with the hair on the outside. When they move about in groups in these rough jerkins with a black stripe across the back, and which covers them from head to foot, they could easily be taken for a herd of some sort walking on their hind legs. When they are on their way to work in the fields or returning from it, one of them generally goes at the head playing a guitar of a flute, and the rest follow him in silence and pensive, adapting themselves to his pace, with an air of innocence and stupidity. However, they by no means lack finesse, and the stupid one would be he who trusted to appearances.

As a general rule they are tall, and their apparel makes them look taller still. Their necks, exposed always to the air, are fine and strongly formed, and their chests, free of tight waistcoats and braces, are wide and well developed; but almost all of them are bow-legged.

The old people and men of mature age, if not handsome to look at, struck us at least as being sincere and of marked integrity. They reminded us of monks, such as we used to imagine them poetically. The younger generation appeared to us to be cruder and of a shameless type that impetuously breaks with parental ties and traditions. Have the clergy really ceased to have any influence in family life for only twenty years?

That is only my impression as a visitor.

CHAPTER II

I have already mentioned that I was trying to discover the secret of the monastic life in places where its traces were so recent. By this I don't mean that I was hoping to find some mysterious facts related to the Cartuja in particular, but I was asking its deserted walls to reveal to me the intimate thoughts of the silent recluses whom they had shut away from the outside world for so many centuries. I would have liked to follow the slender or broken thread of Christian faith in the souls committed there by each generation as a sacrifice to a jealous God, who demanded human victims the same as did the pagan gods. I would have liked, finally, to bring back to life a Carthusian monk of the 15th century, and another of the 19th, and to compare these two Catholics with each other, whose faith would be separated, without their knowing it, by unfathomable depths, and to ask each one what he thought of the other.

It seemed to me that I could easily reconstruct the life of the first one in my imagination, with reasonable accuracy. I saw this Christian of the Middle Ages as a complete personality: pious, sincere, heart-broken at the spectacle of wars, strife and the sufferings of his contemporaries, he fled from this abyss of evil searching in ascetic contemplation for abstraction and for isolation from a life in which the idea of the perfectibility of the masses was in no way attainable by society.

But I couldn't imagine so easily the Carthusian of the 19th century, who shut his eyes to the obvious and irrepressible progress of humanity, indifferent to the life of other men, who didn't even understand either religion, the Pope, the Church, society or himself; who only saw in the Cartuja a spacious residence, pleasant and secure, and in his vocation only an assured existence, an impunity granted to his instincts, and a means for obtaining, without any personal merit, the deference and consideration of the devout, the peasants and the women; him I couldn't place at all. I couldn't assess the remorse he might feel, nor the extent of his blindness, his hypocrisy, nor his sincerity. It is impossible that this man should have had any real faith in the Roman Church, unless he lacked all intelligence. It was also impossible for him to have been a complete atheist, because his life in that case wauld have been an odious lie, and I cannot imagine a man so utterly stupid and base.

Frequently I picture, as a kind of hell, the inner struggles of this imagined person, his alternating fits of rebellion and submission, of philosophical doubt and superstitious terror; and the more I identified myself with the last Carthusian who had occupied my cell before me, the more strongly did I feel his affliction and restlessness weigh upon my impressionable imagination.

It was enough to cast a glance at the old cloisters and at the new part of the Cartuja, to realise how the necessities of comfort, hygiene and even elegance had been gradually introduced into the lives of the hermits, and also to notice the relaxation in monastic customs, and in the spirit of mortification and penitence. Whilst the old cells were gloomy, cramped and draughty, the new ones were light, airy and well built. I will describe the one we lodged in so as to give some idea of the austerity of the Carthusian order, which had been evaded and toned down as much as possible.

The three rooms which made up our cell were spacious,

with elegantly arched ceilings, and ventilated at the back by fretted rose-windows, all different and of a beautiful design. These three habitations were separated from the cloister by a short dark passage ending in a stout oak door. The wall was three feet thick. The central chamber was used for reading, praying and meditation, and its only piece of furniture was a wide seat with a praying-desk and canopy, six to eight feet high, sunk into and fixed to the wall. The chamber to the right was the monk's bedroom, at the back of which there was a very low alcove, paved like a sepulchre. The room to the left was the workshop, refectory and store of the recluse. A closet at the back had a small wooden door which opened onto the cloister rather like a dormer window, and through this food was passed to him. His kitchen consisted of two small cooking-stoves placed outside the room, but not in the open air, as strictly according to rule; for a covered way in the garden protected the monk's culinary activities against the rain, and allowed him to devote rather more time to this occupation than the founder of the Order would have liked. In addition, a fireplace installed in this third room denoted a further relaxation, although the architect had not succeeded in making it of practical use.

The whole appartment had a long, narrow space at the back, at the height of the rose-windows, which was intended for ventilation; and above the cell there was a loft, for the storage of corn, onions, beans and other winter provisions. On the south side, the three rooms opened onto a small garden, of exactly the same length as the cell; this was separated from the neighbouring gardens by a terrace wall rising up from a small orange orchard, which covered this part of the mountain. Lower down the slope there was a vineyard, further on almond trees and palms, and so on successively down to the bottom of the valley, which, as I have already said, was a huge garden.

The garden-plot outside each cell had all along one side, to the right, a cistern made of stone blocks, three or four feet wide by about the same deep, which received water from the mountain via a conduit made in the balustrade of the balcony. From this tank the water was distributed to the little garden by way of stone channels in the form of a cross that divided the plot into four equal parts. I have never heard of a similar water supply for assuaging the thirst of one single man, nor of such extravagant irrigation for a garden twenty feet in diameter. If I hadn't known the particular horror of monks for bathing, together with the frugality of the Majorcans in this respect, I could well have believed that these good Carthusians spent their lives in ablutions, like Indian priests.

This little garden, filled with pomegranate, lemon and orange trees, circumscribed by brick pathways slightly raised above ground level and shaded, like the water cistern, by fragrant climbing plants, looks like a beautiful salon of flowers and verdure, through which the monk could stroll and keep his feet dry on wet days, and refresh the grass with running water when it was hot. Standing at the edge of a splendid balcony, he could breathe the perfume of the orange trees whose dense tops offered to the eye leafy domes resplendent with flowers and fruit. He was able to contemplate in absolute peace a landscape that was at one and the same time austere and gay, melancholy and magnificent, and which I have already spoken about.

He was able to cultivate rare and lovely flowers to delight the eye, and he had within reach the most delicious fruits to quench his thirst. He could listen to the wonderful noises of the sea, gaze at the splendour of the summer nights under the most beautiful sky, and worship the Eternal God in the finest temple open to man in the heart of nature. Such at first sight did the ineffable joys of the Carthusian monk appear to me, and such I vowed I would have when I installed myself in one of those cells, which seemed to have been designed to satisfy the grandiose whims of the imagination, or a host of poetical and artistic dreams.

However, when one pictures to oneself the existence of a man without intelligence, and therefore without dreams and thoughts, perhaps without faith, that is, without enthusiasm or composure, buried in this cell of thick, silent, deaf walls

— when one imagines an existence submitted to the stupefying deprivations of regimentation, obliged to observe the letter of the law without understanding its spirit, condemned to the horrors of solitude, and reduced to glimpsing from the top of a mountain the human race in the distance, moving about at the bottom of the valley — when one thinks of an existence where a man is forced to remain for ever a stranger to other captive souls vowed to the same silence, enclosed in the same tomb, always side by side yet always apart, even in prayer — finally, when one is led by compassion to feel vague fears and misgivings, all this becomes sad and sombre, like a life without substance, a life of error and impotence.

We can understand, then, the immeasurable weariness of this monk for whom the finest spectacles of nature means nothing, for the simple reason that he has no other man with whom to share his enjoyment. We can appreciate too the oppressive sadness of this penitent, who reacts only to the cold and the heat, like an animal or a plant, and the deadly chilliness of this Christian being in whom nothing encourages or revives the spirit of ascetism. Condemned to eat alone, to work alone, to suffer and pray alone, he must feel only one necessity: that of escaping from his dreadful confinement. And I have been told that some of the last Carthusian monks felt no scruples about absenting themselves for weeks and months, without the Prior being able to make them return to their Order.

I am afraid I have written a long and detailed description of the Cartuja, without having given the least idea of how enchanting it was for us at first, and of the extent to which it lost its poetical appeal once we had subjected it to a searching examination. I have concentrated, as I always do, on the main theme of my narrative, and now that I have tried to convey my impressions, I ask myself why I have not been able to express in twenty lines what I have said in twenty pages: "that the carefree repose of the spirit and all that brings it about seems very gratifying and acceptable to a tired soul, but that with reflection the charm disappears". Only a genius has the gift of being able to trace a live and complete

153

picture with a single stroke of the brush. When Lamennais visited the Camaldolites in Tivoli, he had this same feeling and expressed it in masterly fashion:

"We arrived at their convent", he says, "at the hour of common prayer. They all seemed to us to be well advanced in age, and above the normal stature. After the service they remained on their knees in rows on both sides of the aisle, motionless and in deep meditation. One would have said that they no longer belonged to this world; their bald heads were bowed under the weight of different thoughts and cares. Not a movement, not a visible sign of life. Wrapped in their long white mantles, they looked like those statues we see praying on old tombs.

"We can imagine perfectly the kind of attraction which this lonely existence has for certain souls tired of the world, and disabused of their illusions. Who has not at some time aspired for something similar? Who has not turned his eyes more than once towards the wilderness, and dreamed of quietude in a remote corner of the forest, or in a mountain grotto, near an unknown spring where the birds of the sky slake their thirst?

"And yet, this is not the true destiny of man; he has been born for action, he has his duty to fulfil. What does it matter if the task is difficult? Hasn't he also been born for love?" (Affairs of Rome.)

This brief passage, so full of imagination, of aspirations, ideas and profound thoughts, interposed as if by chance in the account of Lamennais's exchanges with the Holy See, has always impressed me, and I am sure that one day it will furnish some painter with the subject for a picture. On one side of it, the Camaldolites at prayer, obscure, peaceful monks, ever purposeless ever impotent, fading spectres and the last manifestations of a cult on the point of sinking into the darkness of the past, and kneeling on the tombstones, as cold and sad-looking as the latter; on the other side, the man of the future, the last priest animated by the last flash of spirit of the Church, meditating on the fate of those monks, looking at them as an artist would, and appraising them like

154

a philosopher. Here, the Levites of death, motionless under their shrouds; there, the apostle of life, an indefatigable traveller through the limitless fields of thought, now bidding a final farewell of sympathy to the poetry of the cloister, and shaking from his feet the dust of the city of the Popes to sally forth along the sacred path of religious freedom.

I have not gathered any other historical data about the Cartuja than that concerning the preaching of the godly Vicente Ferrer, or Ferrier, in Valldemosa. This preaching was the great event in Majorca in 1413, and it is interesting to note how ardently a missionary was wanted at that time, and with what great ceremony he was received.

In the year 1409 the Majorcans, gathered together in a grand assembly, agreed to write to the great Ferrer, to persuade him to come and preach in Majorca. It was Don Luis de Prades, bishop of Majorca, and a chamberlain of the pope Benedict XIII (the antipope Pedro de Luna), who wrote in 1412 a letter to the jurors in Valencia, begging for apostolic assistance from Master Vicente; and it was he who went the next year to meet the preacher in Barcelona and embark with him for Palma. From the day after his arrival the holy missionary began his sermons, and ordered nocturnal processions. There was a very bad drought in the island, but at the third sermon of the great Vicente rain fell. This information was remitted to King Ferdinand by the royal procurator, Don Pedro de Casaldaguila:

"Your Supreme, most Excellent and Victorious Majesty. I have the honour to announce that the learned Vicente has arrived in this city on the 1st September, and has been most ceremonially received. On Saturday morning he began preaching before an immense crowd, who listened to him with devoted attention; and every night there are processions, in which men, women and children can be seen scourging themselves. And as it had not rained for a long time, Our Lord God, moved to compassion by the prayers of the children and of the people, has willed that this kingdom, which was dying from the drought, should see after the third ser-

155

mon rain falling over the whole island, which has very greatly rejoiced the inhabitants.

"May Our Lord God grant you many years of life, Most Victorious Majesty, and bless your royal crown."

"Majorca, 11th September 1413."

The crowd who wished to listen to the holy missionary grew to such an extent that the church of the convent of Santo Domingo couldn't hold them, and it was necessary to make use of the monastery's huge garden, knocking down walls and raising platforms.

Vicente Ferrer preached in Palma until the 3rd October, when he set off to visit the island. His first stop was at Valldemosa, where he was received and lodged in the monastery, and which doubtlessly he had chosen out of consideration for his brother Boniface, the Superior of the Carthusian Order. The Prior of Valldemosa had decided to go personally to Palma to collect him and travel back with him. In Valldemosa, more even than in the capital, the church was too small to contain the avid crowd. Here is what the chroniclers say:

"The town of Valldemosa remembers the time when the godly Vicente Ferrer spread the divine word there. Within the town limits there is a property called Son Gual. The missionary made his way there followed by a prodigious multitude. The ground was flat and covered a wide area; and the hollow trunk of a huge, old olive tree served him as a pulpit. Whilst the holy man was preaching from the top of the olive tree, the rain began to fall heavily. The devil, that promoter of winds, thunder and lightning, seemed bent on forcing the listeners to leave the place and take shelter, which some of them were already commencing to do when Vicente ordered them not to move; he began to pray and immediately a cloud spread like a canopy over him, and over whoever was listening to him; whilst those who had stayed working in the fields nearby were obliged to abandon their labour.

"The old tree trunk was still in existence less than a century ago, for our ancestors had preserved it religiously. Time passed, and as the heirs to Son Gual paid no heed to this sacred object, memory of it faded. However, it was not

156

God's will that Vicente Ferrer's rustic pulpit should disappear for ever. Some servants of the estate wanted to chop firewood, and seeling the olive tree they tried to cut it down; but the tools broke at the first blows, and when the news reached the ears of the old people, they believed it was a miracle, and the hallowed olive tree remained intact. With the passage of time this tree split up into a large number of pieces, and although they were taken into the town, nobody dared to touch them, and they were regarded as á divine relic.

"The holy preacher continued on his way, and went preaching in the smallest villages and healing the bodies and souls of the unfortunate. The water of a spring that flows on the outskirts of Valldemosa was the only remedy prescribed by the saint. This spring is still known by the name of *Sa bassa Ferrera*.

"San Vicente spent six months in the island, from where he was summoned by Ferdinand, king of Aragon, so that he could help him to stamp out the discord that was upsetting the West. The godly missionary took his leave of the Majorcans with a sermon that he preached on the 22nd February 1414, in Palma Cathedral; and after giving his blessing to the congregation he departed to go on board ship, escorted by the jurors, the nobility and the people. He performed many other miracles, as the chroniclers relate, and as tradition has perpetuated down to our present days in the Balearics."

This story, which would make Miss Fanny Elssler[1] smile, gives rise to an observation by Monsieur Tastu, which is curious in two ways; firstly because he explains with great artlessness one of Vicente Ferrer's miracles, and secondly, because he confirms an extraordinary fact in the history of languages. The following are his remarks:

"Vicente Ferrer wrote his sermons in Latin and deliver-

1. One of two well known and very popular Austrian dancers, Thérèse and Fanny Elssler, contemporary with the authoress. *(Translator's note.)*

ed them in Languedocian, or the language of Provençal. This faculty of the saintly preacher has been regarded as a miracle, that he could make himself understood by his listeners in spite of speaking to them in a strange tongue. There is nothing, however, more natural if we bear in mind the times when Master Vicente flourished. In those days the Romance language of the three great regions of the north, the centre and the south, were, with small differences, the same. The ordinary people and the scholars understood each other perfectly. The learned Vicente was successful in England, Scotland, Ireland, Paris, Brittany, Italy, Spain and in the Balearic Islands. And the fact is that he was understood in all these places although people did not speak a Romance language, or any other similar, related or allied to the Valencian language, Vicente Ferrer's mother tongue.

"Besides, wasn't the famous preacher a contemporary of the poet Chaucer, of Jean Froissart, Christine de Pisan, Boccaccio, Ausias March, and of very many other European celebrities?"[2]

---

2. These remarks by M. Tastu, which the author includes to round off the picture, are full of inaccuracies which we don't consider necessary to detail. They are not consistent with M. Tastu's knowledge of languages. (Translator's note.)

CHAPTER III

I cannot continue my narrative without first reproducing an extract from the ecclesiastical records of Valldemosa; for, in emphasizing the fanatical piety of the villagers with whom we were brought into contact, I must make mention of the saint of whom they are so proud, and whose rustic birthplace they showed us:

"Valldemosa is also the home-land of Catalina Tomas, beatified in 1792 by the pope, Pius VI. The life of the saint has been written many times, and latterly by Cardinal Antonio Despuig. It recounts for us many acts of pleasing ingenuousness. The story goes that, having been favoured by God with an intelligence far beyond her years, it was noted that she rigorously observed the days of fasting long before she reached the age prescribed by the Church. From her earliest childhood she abstained from having more than one meal a day. Her devotion to the Passion of the Redeemer and to the Dolours of his Holy Mother was so fervent that she was continually telling her beads during her walks, and making use of the leaves of the olive and mastic trees to count her *Ave Marías*. Her tendency to seclusion and religious exercises, her dislike of dancing and her withdrawal from worldly amusements, caused her to be known as the *viejecita* (the little old woman). But her solitude and her sobriety were rewarded by visits from angels and the entire celestial court. Jesus Christ, His Holy Mother and the Saints became her servitors. Mary nursed her in her illnesses, St. Bruno lifted her up when she fell. St. Anthony accompanied her in the darkness of the night, carrying and filling her pitcher at the fountain. St. Katherine, her patron saint, did her hair for her, and cared for her as any anxious and devoted mother would have done. St. Côme and St. Damien healed the wounds she received in her struggles with the devil, for her victories were not won without fighting; and finally, St. Peter and St. Paul were at her side to help and defend her in her temptations.

"She embraced the Order of St. Augustine in the convent of Santa Magdalena in Palma, being an exemplary penitent and, as the Church chants in its prayers, obedient, poor, chaste and humble. Her biographers attribute to her the powers of prophecy, and the gift of performing miracles. They relate that, at the time when prayers were being said in public for the health of the pope, Pius V, Catalina interrupted them suddenly one day to announce that they were no longer necessary, because at that very instant the pontiff had left this world, which turned out to be true.

"She died on the 5th April 1574, uttering the words of the Psalmist: "Lord, into thy hands I commend my soul."

"Her death was regarded as a public calamity, and she was awarded the highest honours. A pious Majorcan lady, Doña Juana de Pochs, replaced the wooden coffin in which the saint had been laid with another one of magnificent alabaster, which she ordered from Genoa; and in addition, she instituted, through her will, a mass for the day of the passing on of the blessed one, and another for the festival of St. Katherine, her patron saint; she also expressed a wish that a lamp should burn perpetually over Catalina's tomb.

"The body of this godly girl is preserved today in the nun's convent in the parish of Santa Eulalia, where Cardinal

Despuig has consecrated an altar to her and a religious service."[1]

I have gladly transcribed this short account by M. Tastu, because it doesn't enter into my thoughts in any way to deny saintliness, that is to say, the true, genuine saintliness of impassioned persons. Although the enthusiasm and visions of the little country-girl from Valldemosa don't have the same religious meaning and the same philosophical value as the inspirations and emotional transports of the saints in the heyday of Christianity, the *viejecita Tomás* doesn't fail at least to be first cousin of the poetical St. Geneviève or of the sublime shepherdess, Joan of Arc.

At no time has the Roman Church refused to grant places of honour in the kingdom of heaven to the most humble of the sons of the people; but there have been times when it has condemnned and rejected those among the apostles who wished to exalt the place of the people in the kingdom of the earth. The *pagesa* (country-girl) Catalina was "obedient, poor, chaste and humble"; the *pagès* (country-boys) profited so little by her example and knew so little about her life, that one day they wanted to stone my children because my son was sketching the monastery, a thing which seemed to them sacrilegious. They were doing the same as the Church, which lit the bonfires of the Inquisition with one hand, and with the other acclaimed the effigies of its saints and benefactors.

The village of Valldemosa,[2] which has taken pride in calling itself a town since the time of the Moors, is situated on the slope of the mountain, at the same height as the Cartuja, of which it seems to be an annexe. It is a mass of sea-gulls' nests. It is located in an almost inaccessible position, and its inhabitants are for the most part fishermen, who leave for their work in the morning and don't return until night. Dur-

---

1.   The body of Catalina Tomas, now a saint, is kept in the church of the Convent of Santa Magdalena, whose Augustinian community she joined as a choir nun. (*Translator's note.*)

2.   The Arabs called it Villa-Avente, a Roman name, which I believe it received from the Pisans or Genoese. (*Note by Monsieur Tastu.*)

ing the day the village is taken over by the women, the most talkative in the world, who can generally be seen on the doorsteps of the houses, busy mending their husbands' nets or breeches, and singing at the top of their voices without stop. They are as religious as the men, but their religion is less intolerant, because it is more genuine; that is an advantage which they have there, as everywhere, over the opposite sex. In general, the fondness of these women for religious observances stems from sincerity, custom or conviction, whilst in the men it is almost always the product of ambition or self-interest. France offered a clear enough proof of this in the reigns of Louis XVIII and Charles X, when the highest administrative and military posts were obtainable with a confessional note or a mass.

The attachment felt by the Majorcans for monks is founded on motives of avarice, and I cannot explain this better than by quoting the opinion of *Señor Marliani:* an opinion which is all the more to be trusted because the historians of modern Spain mostly appear to be opposed to the measures taken in 1836 in connection with the sudden expulsion of the brothers.

He says, "Benevolent landlords, who were inclined to be a little careless with their money, had created genuine regard between themselves and the country people. The tenant farmers who worked the properties of the monasteries suffered no great hardships in the matter of the amount or regularity of their rent payments. The friars, having no future, saved nothing; and as soon as they had enough of the world's goods to satisfy the material needs of each one, they were very generous with what was left over. The forcible expropriation of the monks, therefore, upset the calculations, idle dreams and egoism of the country folk, who realised at once that the government and new owners would be more exigent than a parasitical community without family or social interests. The beggars who milled around the doors of the monastery's refectory no longer received the left-overs of those well-filled drones".

The Carlism of the Majorcan country people can only be

162

explained by purely materialistic reasons; for it is impossible otherwise to find a province less united to Spain by patriotic feelings, nor a people less inclined to political agitation. Despite the secret vows they made to restore old customs and practices, they nevertheless were appalled at the thought of any change whatever it might be; and the emergency which had put the island into a state of siege at the time we stayed there, frightened both the adherents of Don Carlos in Majorca, and the supporters of Queen Isabel. The emergency was something that brought out very clearly, I will not say the cowardice of the Majorcans, for I believe they can be very good soldiers, but the general anxiety caused by worrying about their property, and their self-centred desire for peace and quiet.

An old priest dreamed one night that his house was being broken into by robbers. He awoke, terrified by his nightmare, got up and roused his servant. The latter, sharing his master's terror and not knowing what it was all about, woke up the whole neighbourhood with his shouts. Fear spread quickly through the village, and from there to the whole island. News of the landing of the Carlist army gripped everyone's mind. The Captain-General received the report of the priest who, either ashamed to retract or still scared out of his wits, affirmed that he had seen the Carlists. A state of siege was declared in Palma, and all the military forces of the island were put on a war footing.

However, nobody appeared; not a bush nor a bramble stirred; no strange footprint was found in the sand on the beach, as in Robinson Crusoe's island. The authorities severely reprimanded the wretched priest, and instead of sending him packing as being out of his mind, they imprisoned him as if he was a seditious person. But the precautionary measures were not relaxed, and when we left Majorca at the time of Maroto's executions, the state of siege was still on in the island.

There is nothing stranger than the kind of mystery with which the Majorcans seemed to like passing on from one to another what was happening at that time in Spain and upsett-

163

ing the whole country. Nobody spoke about it, unless in his own home and in a low voice. In a place where there really is no wickedness or tyranny, it is unbelievable to see such gloomy mistrust reigning. I have read nothing so amusing as the articles in the Palma daily paper, and I have always regretted not having brought some of the copies with me, as examples of Majorcan polemics. But here, without exaggeration, is the manner in which, after reporting the facts, their authenticity and import are commented on:

"However true these reports may appear in the eyes of those ready to believe them, we cannot recommend our readers too strongly that they should await events before passing judgment on them. Such matters deserve mature consideration on our part, while we are waiting for a confirmation of which there can be no doubt, but which neither can we assume to be true in a hasty and imprudent manner. The destinies of Spain are cloaked in a veil which will be lifted ere long, but on which no one must put an indiscreet hand before the proper time. Until then we will abstain from passing an opinion, and we advise all sensible persons not to comment on the acts of the different parties until the situation is delineated in a clearer fashion, etc., etc..."

Prudence and reserve are, by the Majorcans' own confession, the predominant traits in their character. The peasants never meet you in the country without exchanging a greeting with you; but if you try to get into conversation, and they don't know you, they are very guarded in their replies, although you may speak to them in their same language. It's enough for you to look like a foreigner for them to distrust you, and turn aside to avoid you.

Anyway, we could have lived in peace with these good people if we had attended their church. They wouldn't have stopped gossiping about us on every possible occasion, but we would have been able to walk through their fields without running the risk of having a stone thrown at our heads from behind some bush. Unfortunately this act of prudence didn't occur to us at the beginning of our stay there, and we were unaware almost until the end of how much our way of life shocked them. They called us heathens, Mahommedans and Jews, which, according to them, is the worst thing one can be. The Mayor warned the persons under his jurisdiction against us, and I am not sure that the parish priest didn't take us as a text in his sermons. My daughter's shirt and trousers also greatly scandalized them; they thought it very wrong that a young girl should roam around the mountain "disguised as a man". And it was not only the peasants who affected this prudery.

The trumpet which resounded on Sundays in the village and along the roads to warn the loiterers that it was time to go to church, pursued us in vain in the Cartuja. At first we took no notice of it because we didn't know what it was about, but when we did realise we took even less notice. Then they found a way of avenging the glory of God, a way which was not at all Christian. They leagued together and agreed among themselves not to sell us fish, eggs and vegetables except at exorbitant prices. It was no use our quoting tariffs or the usual charges. At the least observation the peasant would put his onions or potatoes back into the sack, and say to us with the air of a Grandee of Spain. "Do you not want them? Then you will not have them"; and he would retire in a highly dignified fashion, without our being able to make him return and come to an agreement. They made us go short in order to punish us for bargaining with them.

We did really go short. There was no competition or price reduction among the vendors. The second one who came along asked double, and the third one treble, so that we found ourselves at their mercy, and we led the lives of hermits, only more expensive than the life of a prince in Paris would have been. We did, however, have the recourse of supplying ourselves in Palma through the consul's chef, who was our saviour and whose cotton cap, if I was a Roman Emperor, I would include among the stars. But on rainy days no carrier would risk himself on the road at any price, and as it rained for two months we often had bread as hard as a ship's biscuit and veritable Carthusian style meals.

165

This would have been of insignificant annoyance if all of us had enjoyed good health. I myself am quite moderate and indifferent by nature with regard to food. The splendid appetites of my children turned anything into a savoury feast and a simple, green lemon into a delicacy. My son, whom I had taken there weak and sickly, recuperated as though by a miracle and shook off a very serious rheumatic affection, running from very early morning like a hunted hare through the thickets on the mountain, often soaked to the skin. Providence permitted nature to work these wonders in him. But we now had enough with an invalid on our hands.

The latter, far from improving in the damp air and lack of necessities, became distressingly worse. Although he had been reported on adversely by the doctors in Palma, he was not suffering from any chronic ailment; but the lack of a sustaining diet had left him, after an attack of catarrh, in a state of languor from which he couldn't rouse himself; he resigned himself, as one knows can happen, to his seedy condition. But we had to keep going, and for the first time I began to be seriously upset by quite minor pin-pricks: for instance, my anger over a broth that was too highly seasoned, or "pinched" by the servants, and my anxiety about some new bread that didn't arrive, or had been turned into a sponge while being transported across a torrent on the back of a mule. I cannot remember at all what I ate in Pisa or Trieste; but if I live to be a hundred, I shall never forget the arrival of the provision basket at the Cartuja. What I would not have given to be able to offer our invalid every day a bowl of soup and a glass of Bordeaux! The Majorcan food, and especially the manner in which it was spiced, always caused him a malaise unless we supervised it ourselves. Up to what point was this justified? All I can say is that one day when we were served with a skinny chicken we saw hopping about on its steaming back some enormous "Maîtres Floh",[3] which Hoffman would have described as so many malign spirits,

---

3. Fowl fleas. This expression may refer to one of Hoffman's tales or his opera *Undine*. (*Translator's note.*)

but which he certainly wouldn't have eaten with gravy. My children roared with such infantile laughter that they nearly fell under the table.

The basis of Majorcan cooking is, invariably, the pig, in all its shapes and forms. It would be opportune here to quote the remark made by the little Savoyard when he was boasting about his larder; looking at his listeners, he said that five different kinds of meat could be eaten, namely: pig, pork, lard, ham and bacon. I am sure that in Majorca they make more than two thousand kinds of dishes, and at least two hundred species of sausages, seasoned with such a profusion of garlic, pepper, cayenne and corrosive spices of every sort, that one risks one's life with every mouthful.

If you see appear on the table twenty dishes that seem to contain all kinds of normal food, you must not, however, trust them, for they will be infernal drugs cooked by the devil in person. Finally comes the dessert, an innocent-looking pastry tart with pieces of fruit that look like candied oranges; that's all right; but it happens to be a bacon tart, with garlic, slices of tomatoes and peppers, all sprinkled with white salt, which from its harmless aspect you mistake for sugar. Chickens abound, but they are all skin and bone. In Valldemosa it would have cost us at least a real (an old Spanish silver coin) for each grain of corn we bought to fatten them. The fish they brought us from the sea was as thin and dry as the poultry.

One day we bought a fair-sized octopus in order to have the pleasure of examining it. Never have I seen such a horrible creature. Its body was as big as a turkey's, its eyes the size of oranges, and its flaccid and repulsive tentacles measured four or five feet. The fishermen assured us that it was a tasty morsel, but we were put off by its looks, so we presented it to Maria Antonia, who cooked and dressed it, and found it delicious.

If our admiration for the octopus made these good people smile, we also had the opportunity a few days later to smile at them in our turn. Coming down the mountain we saw the "pagès" leaving their work and hurrying towards a group of people who had stopped on the road, and who were carrying in a basket a pair of extraordinary, marvellous and unidentifiable birds. Everybody on the mountain was in a state of excitement at the appearance of the unknown winged wonders.

Some said as they looked at them:

"What do these animals eat?" And others replied, "Perhaps they don't eat anything". "Do they live on the land or on the sea?" "Probably they always live in the air."

The two birds, which looked on the point of being stifled by the public admiration they were receiving, were neither condors, phoenixes nor hippogriffs; they were simply two magnificent, domestic geese which a rich gentleman was sending as a gift to a friend of his.

In Majorca, as in Venice, liqueurs are plentiful and very fine. Ordinarily we drank a muscatel as good and as cheap as the Cyprus wine which is drunk on the Adriatic littoral. But the red wines, whose manufacture is a veritable art unknown to the Majorcans, are rough, black coloured, fiery, strongly alcoholic, and more expensive than the commonest table wine in France. All these pungent and intoxicating wines were very harmful for our invalid, and obnoxious also to us, so that we almost always drank the water, which was excellent. I don't know if it was due to the purity of this spring water that we must attribute something we noticed very soon: our teeth acquired a whiteness that all the arts of the perfumers in Paris couldn't give to their most fastidious customers. It is possible that the reason lay in our enforced frugality.

Lacking butter, and unable to put up with the lard, the nauseating oil and burnt methods of the native cooking, we lived on very lean meat, fish and vegetables, all seasoned, not with sauce, but with water from the torrent, to which we permitted ourselves the luxury of adding the juice of a green orange, freshly picked from our small garden. On the other hand, we had some excellent desserts: sweet potatoes from Malaga, pickled pumkins from Valencia, and grapes that might have come from the land of Canaan. The latter fruit, white or pink, is oblong and covered with a thickish film that helps to preserve it during the whole year. It is delicious and you can eat as much as you like without fear of getting the heaviness of stomach that ours give. The Fontainebleau grape is juicier and fresher; the Majorcan variety is sweeter and more pulpy. The latter has to be eaten, the former can be drunk. The bunches (there are some which weigh from twenty to twenty-five pounds) would have been a delight for a painter. The grape was our means of sustenance in times of scarcity. The local people thought they were selling them to us very dear, and they did make us pay four times their proper price, but they didn't realise that, compared with ours in France, the cost was very cheap; and so we had the pleasure of befooling each other. In regard to the prickly pears there was no argument; it is the most horrible fruit I know.

If the circumstances of this frugal existence hadn't been, I repeat, harmful and even disastrous for one of us, the rest of us would have been able to put up with it quite well. We had succeeded, even in Majorca, even in an abandoned Carthusian monastery, and at loggerheads with the most artful country people in the world, in creating for ourselves a fair degree of comfort. We had glass windows, doors and a stove; a unique stove of its kind, which the best blacksmith in Palma took a month to make, and which cost us a hundred francs. It consisted simply of an iron cylinder with a pipe that led out through the window; it took an hour to light it, and it had hardly got going when it became red-hot, so that we had first to open the doors to let out the smoke, and then open them again to let out the heat. Besides this, the so-called bricklayer had lined the interior of the fireplace with the material that the Indians use to coat their houses and even their persons, bearing in mind that the cow there is a sacred animal. However purifying this saintly odour may be for the soul, I can testify that the heat of the fire holds little delight for the senses. During the month it took for this mortar to dry out, we could imagine ourselves to be in that gathering in hell where Dante claims he saw the devil's

169

worshippers. I searched my memory in vain for what sin I had done that deserved such torture, what power on earth I had incensed, what pope or king I had encouraged in their errors by my flattery. I hadn't on my conscience either an office-boy or a page-boy, not even a blandishment to a gendarme or a journalist.

Luckily, the Carthusian pharmacist was able to sell us a very fine benzoin, or aromatic resin, from the remains of the stock of perfumes which were used not so long ago for incense before the divine image in the monastery church; and this heavenly aroma effectively counteracted the hellish emanations in our cell.

We had magnificent furniture, excellent beds, fairly soft mattresses, dearer than in Paris but new and clean, and some of those big calico quilts which the Jews sell in Palma quite cheaply. A French lady living in the island was kind enough to give us a quantity of feathers which she had ordered to be sent out from Marseilles, and with this we made two pillows for our patient. This certainly was a great luxury in a place where geese are looked upon as fantastic creatures, and where the chickens itch even when they come off the spit.

We had several tables, and rush chairs similar to those to be seen in our country cottages, and a luxurious sofa of white wood with coarse cloth cushions stuffed with wool. The floor of the cell, which was very dusty and uneven, was covered with those Valencian mats made with long lengths of straw and look like a patch of turf gilded by the sun; we also had some beautiful long-haired sheepskin rugs of a wonderful fineness and whiteness, which they are experts at making in the country.

As is the case with Africans and Orientals, there are no cupboards in the old Majorcan houses, and especially in the cells of the Carthusian monks. Generally, personal effects are kept in big white wooden trunks. Our yellow leather suitcases could pass there as very elegant pieces of furniture. A very large tartan travelling rug, which we had used during the journey, was turned into a sumptuous curtain across the alcove, and my son decorated the stove with a very attractive large earthenware jar from Felanitx, whose shape and design was in pure Arabic style.

Felanitx is a Majorcan country town which deserves the monopoly of supplying Europe with its beautiful jars, which are so light that you would think they were made of cork, and of such a fine grain that you could mistake the clay with which they are manufactured for some precious material. Small pitchers are made there, of an exquisite design, which are used as carafes and keep the water in a condition of wonderful freshness. The clay is so porous that the water seeps through the sides of the jug, and in less than half a day it is empty. I confess that I don't understand a word about physics, and perhaps my last remark is worse than silly; but to me it seemed marvellous, and my earthenware jug little short of magical. We used to leave it full of water on the stove whose top was usually almost red-hot, and although sometimes the water all escaped through the pores and it remained dry on the burning hot iron plate, it never broke, Whilst there was a drop of water in it, it was as cold as ice, though the heat of the stove blackened any firewood we put on top of it.

This handsome jug, enclosed in a garland of ivy taken from the outer wall, would have satisfied the eyes of an artist more than all our modern Sèvres pottery. The upright Pleyel[4] piano, rescued from the hands of the customs officers after three weeks of argument and payment of four hundred francs in duty, filled the high, arched, re-echoing cell with a magnificent sound. Finally, the sacristan had agreed to move to our cell a beautiful, Gothic box-chair of carved oak wood, which the rats and worms were gnawing in the old church of the Carthusians. The box part of this chair served us as an improvised library, and at night time the lamp cast lovely reflections on the wall, showing up the rich lace-like pattern

4. At the present time in cell number 4 in the Cartuja. (*Translator's note.*)

of the carving, and restored to the cell its former monastic atmosphere.

Señor Gomez, our former landlord of Son Vent, the rich personage who had let his house to us in secret because it wasn't becoming for a citizen of Majorca to speculate with his property, had created a rumpus and threatened us with a lawsuit for having broken some earthenware plates, for which he charged us as if they were Chinese porcelain. He also made us pay, again with threats, for the whitewashing and plastering of the whole of his house, to remove the risk of catching cold by contagion. Anyway, it's an ill wind that blows no good, because he hastened to sell us all the house linen which he had rented us; but, although he was eager to get rid of everything we had touched, he didn't forget to haggle until we had paid for it as though it was new. However, thanks to him, we weren't forced to sow a crop of flax in order one day to have sheets and cloths, as a certain Italian once did so that he could provide his servants with shirts.

You must not accuse me of childishness because I write about all these causes of annoyance, for which I haven't retained a shadow of resentment; but nobody will deny that it is the people who form the most interesting study in a country; and I have to affirm that I hadn't a single financial dealing, however trivial, with the Majorcans without their showing a very obvious bad faith and a gross cupidity. Furthermore, when they displayed their religious fervour for our benefit, affecting to be scandalized by our lack of faith, you will agree with me that piety in such simple people, so extolled by some of our conservative elements these days, isn't always the most edifying and moral thing in the world, and that one must be permitted to hope that there are other ways of understanding and honouring God.

As for myself, I am tired of hearing about these commonplace ideas: that it is a crime and even a danger to attack an erroneous and corrupt faith, because there is nothing to put in its place; that those who are not infected with the poison

172

of philosophical examination and revolutionary madness are the only moral, charitable and sincere people; that they still have poetry, greatness and ancient virtues, etc., and so on... I confess I have laughed, and a little more in Majorca than elsewhere, at these ponderous claims. When I looked at my children, brought up in complete disregard of the conventions, serving and gladly helping a sick friend, they alone among a hundred and sixty thousand Majorcans, who would have turned away with the utmost cruelty and in the most cowardly terror of an illness supposed to be contagious, I told myself that these small villains had more courage and charity than that whole population of saints and apostles.

These pious servants of God said that I was committing a great crime in exposing my children to contagion, and that, to punish me for my folly, heaven would send them the same disease. I answered them that, in our family, if one had the plague, the others would not leave him alone in bed; for it was not the custom in France, neither before nor after the revolution, to abandon sick persons; that Spanish prisoners afflicted with worse and more pernicious complaints, had passed through our country in the time of the Napoleonic wars, and that our peasants, after sharing their bowl of soup and their clothes with them, had given them a bed and remained at their side to look after them; that many of the country people had been victims of their zeal and had succumbed to the contagion, which had not stopped the survivors from continuing to practise hospitality and charity. The Majorcan would shake his head and smile pityingly. The idea of self-sacrifice towards an unknown person could not penetrate his brain, the same as probity and kindness towards a foreigner.

All travellers who have visited the interior of the island have been surprised, however, by the hospitality and impartiality of the Majorcan farmer. They have written appreciatively that, although there were no lodgings to be found in this part of the country, it was none the less easy and enjoyable to travel through the rural areas, where "a simple introduction" was enough to be received, housed and entertained

173

gratuitously. This "simple introduction" is, in my opinion, a fact of considerable importance. These travellers have forgotten to mention that all classes in Majorca, in other words all the inhabitants, have a unity of interests that establishes good and easy relations between them, into which, nevertheless, neither religious charity nor human sympathy enter. A few words about the monetary situation will explain this.

The nobility are rich in landed property, but poor in regard to income, and ruined through having to borrow. The Jews, numerous in number and having plenty of ready cash, hold all the lands of the gentry in pawn, and it can be said in fact that the whole island belongs to them. These gentry are nothing more than aristocratic figureheads, taken up with entertaining each other, as well as any rare foreigners who arrive in the island, on their estates and in their palaces. But even to carry out these lofty functions in a fitting manner, they have to have recourse every year to the purse-strings of the Jews, and so, every year, the snowball grows. I have already described the way in which the revenue from the soil is paralysed on account of the lack of markets and manufactures. However, there is a point of honour among these gentlemen, and that is to accomplish their ruin slowly and quietly, without giving up the luxury, or better, the reckless extravagance of their forefathers. The money-lenders therefore have a permanent financial interest in the agriculturists, from whom they receive part of the farm rent by virtue of the title-deeds handed over to them by the gentry.

Thus the countryman, who perhaps finds some advantage in this division of his debts, pays his landlord as little as he can, and his banker as much as possible. The landlord is complaisant and resigned; the Jew patient but inexorable. He makes concessions, affects a great tolerance and gives time to pay, for he pursues his end with a diabolical genius. From the moment he gets his claws on a property, it is inevitable that bit by bit it will fall completely into his hands; and his object is to make himself so indispensable that finally the debt equals the total value of the property. Within twenty years there will not be a stately home left in Majorca. The

174

Jews there will be able to establish themselves in a position of power, as they have done in our country, and brazen it out, albeit with head still slightly bowed and hypocritically humble, despite the badly dissembled scorn of the nobility, and the puerile and impotent aversion of the workers. Meanwhile they are the true owners of the land, and the country people fear and distrust them. The peasant is concerned, therefore, in satisfying and even humouring two masters, so as not to be crushed between them.

Have an introduction, then, to a countryman, either from a lord or from someone rich (and from whom else could it be when there is no middle class?), and every door will be opened at once for you. But try asking for a glass of water without an introduction, and you will see what happens.

And yet for all that, the Majorcan countryman is gentle, kind, peaceful, and has a calm and patient disposition. He doesn't like evil, but he doesn't know good. He confesses, prays and dreams of going to heaven, but he is ignorant of the proper duties of mankind. He is no worse than an ox or a sheep, for he is scarcely more man than the creature dormant in the animal's brain. He recites prayers, and is as superstitious as a savage, but he would eat his fellow-being without much regret, if that was the custom and pig's meat was short. He deceives, lies, insults and robs without the least scruple of conscience. A foreigner for him is not a man. He would never steal an olive from a compatriot; but beyond the seas humanity only exists in the designs of God to bring gain and advancement to the Majorcans.

We have nicknamed Majorca the "Island of Monkeys", for we seemed to be surrounded by these mangy, plundering, yet innocent animals; however we managed to keep away from them without feeling any more rancour or animosity than that caused to the Indians by the orang-outangs and the miscievous, elusive baboons.

Nevertheless, no one, without feeling sadness, can get used to seeing creatures, clothed in human form and marked with the divine seal, existing in circumstances that are unbefitting of present-day humanitarianism. We well know that this imperfect being is capable of understanding, that its breed is capable of improvement, that its future is the same as the most advanced types, and that this is only a question of time, long in our eyes but insignificant in the span of eternity. But the more one has this feeling about its capacity for development, the more one grieves at seeing it so chained to the past. This standstill in time, which is scarcely noticed by the Deity, distresses and saddens our daily existence. We feel in our hearts, in our minds, in our innermost being, that the lives of all others are linked to ours, that we cannot do without loving and being loved, without understanding and being understood, without helping or being helped. The feeling of a moral and intellectual superiority over other men only satisfies the heart of the proud. I imagine all generous hearted people would like, not to lower themselves to inferior standards, but to bring those on a lower level up to their own as quickly as possible, with the object of living at last a true life of sympathy, friendly relationship, equality and mutual help, which is the religious ideal of the human conscience.

I am certain that this desire lies at the bottom of every heart, and that those of us who combat it and believe they can stifle it with sophisms feel a strange and bitter pain to which they cannot give a name. Men of the lower classes decline and fade away when they can't better themselves; those of higher station in life become indignant and distressed when you vainly try to give them a helping hand; and those who don't want to help anybody are consumed with boredom and fear of solitude, until they finally fall into a stupor which reduces them to a lower level than that reached by the first-named.

CHAPTER IV

W E were, then, alone in Majorea, as alone as in a desert, and when our daily subsistence had been assured, after warring with the "monkeys", the family assembled round the stove to make fun of it all. But as winter advanced, sadness paralysed all my heartfelt efforts at gaiety and calmness. The condition of our invalid grew steadily worse; the wind howled down the ravine, the rain lashed our windows, the thunderclaps sounded through our thick walls and interjected a lugubrious note into the children's laughter and games. The eagles and hawks, emboldened by the mist, came down and snatched away our poor sparrows from the pomegranate tree right in front of my very window. The stormy sea kept the boats in the harbour; we felt like prisoners, far away from all intelligent help and any kind of proper friendliness.

Death seemed to be hovering over our heads ready to alight on one of us, and we were alone in our struggle to ward it off its prey. On the contrary, there was not a single human creature around us who would not have liked to hasten him to his grave, and so finish as quickly as possible with the supposed danger of his proximity. The thought of this hostility was terribly sad. With care and sacrifice, we felt strong enough to provide the help and sympathy which was denied us; what is more, I believe that in such trials the heart expands and love is magnified, fortified by all the strength that accrues from a sense of human unity. But we were deeply distressed at finding ourselves thrown amongst people who didn't understand such a sentiment, and for whom we couldn't help feeling pity, rather than our being the object of theirs.

In addition, I was afflicted with intense perplexity. I have no knowledge whatever of the rudiments of medical science, and I would have had to be a doctor, and a very good doctor too, to take charge of the case. The responsibility of it all weighed heavily on my heart.

The doctor who visited us, and on whose zeal and skill I am casting no doubt, was mistaken, as every doctor, including the most brilliant, can be mistaken; just the same as any honest learned person, as he himself admits, can often be deceived. The original bronchitis had been succeeded by a nervous irritation which produced some of the symptoms of a consumptive laryngitis.

The doctor, who had seen these symptoms on certain occasions but had not seen what I had at other times, recommended treatment as for a tubercular patient: bleeding, dieting and milk foods. All these things had completely adverse effects, and the bleeding would have been fatal. The sick man knew it instinctively and I, who had nursed many ill people without knowing anything about medicine, felt the same misgivings. However, I was afraid of being let down by my intuition, and of going against the opinion of a professional man; and when I saw our patient getting worse, I became the prey of great anxiety, as anyone can well understand. "A blood-letting will save him", they told me, "and if you don't agree that we do it, he will die". Yet there was a voice inside me which said, "A blood-letting will kill him, if you can prevent it he will recover". I am persuaded that that voice was the voice of God. And now that our friend, the terror of the Majorcans, has been declared to be about as tubercular as I am, I thank Heaven for not losing the confidence that saved us.

In regard to the diet, it was abhorrent to him, and when we saw its bad consequences we kept to it as little as possible; but unfortunately our choice only lay between the hot spices of the country and an extremely frugal table. Milk food, whose pernicious effects on the invalid we noticed at once, was, luckily, so scarce in Majorca, that we could hardly get any. We were still thinking at that time that ordinary milk would work wonders, and we strove very hard to get it. There are no cows on those mountains, and the goat's milk that was sold to us was always drunk on the way by the boys who brought it to us; but this didn't prevent the jug, when it reached us, being as full as when it left the farm. It was a miracle which the pious errand boys performed every morning, after taking care to say their prayers beside the fountain in the courtyard of the Cartuja.

To put an end to this phenomenon we procured a goat. It was the gentlest and nicest creature in the world: a beautiful little, long-haired, buff coloured African goat, hornless, and with a very crooked nose and drooping ears. These animals differ a lot from ours. They have the coat of a deer and the outline of a sheep; but they lack the frolicsome, mischievous look of our young goats; by contrast, they seem to be full of melancholy. They differ further from the French animals in that they have very small udders and give little milk. When they are in the prime of life, their milk has a sour, rough taste, which the Majorcans thought highly of, but which to us was awful.

Our friendly animal in the Cartuja was in its first maternity. It was hardly two years old and its milk was rather thin; but she was extremely sparing with it, especially when, separated from the flock with which she was accustomed not to gambol (she was too serious, too Majorcan for that), but to wander dreamily round the mountain tops, she fell into a state of dejection that was not without analogy to ours. However there was a lot of grass in the courtyard, and aromatic plants, cultivated a little while ago by the monks, which grew among the little gutters in our garden. Yet nothing consoled her for her captivity. She wandered lost and discon-

179

*12

solate through the cloisters, uttering bleats mournful enough to move the stones to pity. For a companion we gave her a fat sheep, whose thick, white wool was six inches long, one of those sheep which in our country are only to be seen in the windows of toy-shops or on our grandmothers' fans. This excellent companion quietened our goat down somewhat, and also gave us some very creamy milk. But the quantity we obtained from both animals was so little, in spite of being well fed, that we began to suspect the frequent visits that Maria Antonia, the *nina* and Catalina made to them; in the end we decided to put them under lock and key in a small yard at the foot of the bell-tower, and we took care to milk them ourselves. This milk, which was very light, mixed with the milk of the almonds crushed by my children and myself, made a very pleasant, healthy medicinal drink. We couldn't take any other; all the drugs obtainable in Palma were intolerably nasty. The badly refined sugar imported from the Spanish mainland is black, oily, and has purgative qualities for anyone not used to it.

One day we thought we were saved, because we discovered some violets in the garden of a rich farmer. He allowed us to pick some to make a potion, and when we had gathered what we wanted, he made us pay for them at the rate of a *sueldo* per violet, a Majorcan sueldo, which is worth three French sous.

To these domestic activities was added the necessity of sweeping our rooms and making our beds ourselves, if we wanted to sleep at night, for the Majorcan servant woman couldn't touch them without imparting to them at once, with intolerable profusion, the same hopping objects which had so delighted my children, when they saw them on the back of a roast chicken. There were few hours left for us to work and to go out, but they were well employed. The children were attentive at their lessons, and we had only to put our noses outside our door to enter immediately a most varied and wonderful countryside. At every step, in the vast framework of the mountains, there appeared a picturesque undulation in the ground, a small chapel perched on a steep cliff,

180

a thicket of wild strawberry bushes descending almost vertically down a rugged slope, a hermitage close to a spring amongst tall reeds, or a clump of trees amid huge lumps of mossy, ivy-covered rocks. When the sun deigned to appear for a moment, all these plants, rocks, and land washed by the rain took on a magnificent colour.

In particular, we had two unforgettable walks. The first one I don't like to remember, although it was magnificent in many ways, for our invalid, who was then perfectly well (it was the beginning of our stay in Majorca) insisted on going with us, and he tired himself out to such an extent that it brought on the start of his illness.

Our aim was to visit a hermitage situated down by the sea, three miles from the Cartuja. We followed the right arm of the mountain range and climbed in a northerly direction from hill to hill by a stony path that bruised our feet. At every bend of the track we had wonderful views of the sea far down below us and over the most beautiful vegetation. It was the first time that I had seen the fertile shore, covered in trees and green as far as the eye could see, with no bare cliffs, miry beaches or desolate sand dunes. On the coasts of France, even on the heights of Port-Vendres, from where I once had a lovely view of the shore, the sea seemed to me to be dirty and its proximity unpleasant. The Lido, so extolled in Venice, has terribly bare stretches of sand, infested with enormous lizards which appear by the thousand under your very feet, and seem to pursue you in increasing numbers like a nightmare. In Royant, near Marseilles, and I believe on all our coasts, a belt of viscous seaweed and barren sand disfigures the sea approaches. In Majorca, I was able to contemplate the ocean such as I had dreamed it to be, as crystal-clear and blue as the sky, gently rippled like a plain of sapphire carved with regular furrows whose movement is scarcely perceptible seen from a certain height, and bordered by woods of a dark green. Every step we took on the sinuous mountain brought us a new vista more enchanting than the one before. However, as we had to descend in order to arrive at the hermitage, the shore at this particular spot, although pretty enough, didn't have for me the same atmosphere of grandeur that I found on another part of the coast months later.

There was nothing poetically romantic about the four or five hermits who lived in the hermitage. Their dwelling is as wretched and rough as their calling. We found them occupied in digging a terraced garden, from where the immense solitude of the sea stretched away before their eyes. They were not wearing religious robes, and they seemed to us to be the most stupid sort of people in the world. The superior left his spade and came towards us, dressed in a round jacket of dark grey cloth. There was nothing picturesque about his short hair and dirty beard. He spoke to us about the austerity of the life they led, and especially about how unbearably cold it was on that part of the coast. But when we asked him if it ever froze, we were unable to make him understand what frost was. He didn't know the word in any language, and had never heard of countries colder than the island of Majorca. Nevertheless he had some idea of France, because he had seen the French fleet sail by in 1830 on its way to the conquest of Algiers, which he confessed had been the finest, most amazing and unique sight in his life; he asked us if the French had taken Algiers, and when we replied that they had captured Constantine, he opened his eyes wide and affirmed that the French were a great people.

He took us up to a small, very dirty cell, where we met the oldest member of the fraternity. We thought he was a centenarian and were surprised to learn that he was only eighty. He was a complete imbecile, although he was still working mechanically making wooden spoons with his soiled, shaky hands. He took no notice of us, although he was not deaf. The Prior called to him, and he turned to us a hideous, degenerate face. On his distorted countenance there was engraved a life of utter intellectual abasement, and I averted my eyes from him in an instinctive reaction, as being one of the most horrible and distressing objects in the world. We gave them alms, for the friars belong to a begging Order. They enjoy great veneration among the country people, who

182

see that they don't lack for anything. On the way back to the Cartuja we were assailed by a gale from the sea that nearly bowled us over several times, and made our walk so tiring that our invalid was completely exhausted.

Our second unforgettable walk took place a few days before our departure from Majorca, and made such an impression on me that I shall never forget it as long as I live. Never has a piece of natural scenic splendour gripped me more, and I don't think I have seen anything like it more than two or three times in my whole life.

At last the rain had stopped and Spring drew near quite suddenly. We were in February. All the almond trees were in blossom, and the fields were full of sweet-smelling jonquils. This, except for the colour of the sky and the brightness of the countryside, was the only difference that one's eye could detect between the two seasons, for the trees in this region are for the most part evergreens. Those which come into leaf early run no risk from frost; the grass keeps all its freshness, and the flowers only need a morning's sun to stand up to the wind. When half a foot of snow fell in our garden, it rocked our trellised arbours and their pretty climbing roses; but these, belying their pale colour, appeared to weather the storm well.

As on the north side I could discern the sea from the door of the monastery, one day when our invalid was well enough to be left alone for two or three hours, my children and I set off down the road in order to be able to look at the sea-shore from that side. Up to then, I hadn't felt the least curiosity to see it, although my children, who ran about like mountain goats, had assured me that it was the most beautiful sight in the world. Whether the aforementioned visit to the hermitage, the cause of our misfortunes, had left me with a very deep-seated resentment, or, having seen such a beautiful stretch of sea from the top of the mountain, I wasn't keen on contemplating it from the flat, I had not as yet felt tempted to leave the sheltered valley of Valldemosa.

I have said previously that at the point where the Cartuja stands, the cordillera divides, and that a gently sloping plain stretches away between these two branches of the mountain range towards the sea. Very well; but when I saw every day that sea on the horizon appeared to be well above this plain, my eyesight and my reasoning committed a very singular error. Instead of observing that the plain rose and suddenly stopped doing so only a very short distance away, I imagined that it descended in a gentle slope towards the sea, and that the coast was about five or six leagues away. How was I to realise, in fact, that this sea which seemed to be on the same level as the Cartúja, was two or three thousand feet below it? At times I was amazed that its murmur was so loud, being so far off, as I supposed it to be. I couldn't understand the phenomenon, and I don't know how I dare sometimes poke fun at the citizens of Paris, when I was more than stupid in my surmises. I didn't see that that maritime horizon along which I cast my eyes was fifteen or twenty leagues from the coast, whilst the sea pounded the shore of the island a bare half-hour away by road from the Cartúja. So, when my children used to try to persuade me to go and look at the sea-shore, saying that it was only a few steps away, I would say I hadn't time to do it, believing that it was a question of a child's steps, that is to say, in reality, giant's steps; for we know of course that children walk with their imagination, without ever remembering that they have feet, and that the seven league boots of Tom Thumb are a myth to make children think they can go round the world without noticing it.

In the end I was prevailed upon to accompany them, with the foregone certainty that we would never reach that fantastic sea-shore which seemed to me so far off. My son assured me he knew the way, but that means nothing when one walks in seven league boots, and as I hadn't walked in anything but very light shoes for a long time, I warned him I couldn't jump hedges, ditches and torrents like he and his sister. After a quarter of an hour's walking I noticed we were not descending to the sea, for the water in the streams was flowing rapidly towards us, and the farther we progressed the sea appeared to submerge and sink lower and lower on the horizon. Finally I was certain we had turned our backs on it, and I decided to ask the first peasant we met if it was possible, by chance, to find our way down to the coast.

Under a group of willow trees, in a marshy ditch, three small shepherd women, maybe three disguised fairies, were turning the mud over with shovels searching for heaven knows what. The first one had one tooth; she was probably the fairy "Dentue", the same one who stirs her evil concoctions in a stewpan with her single, ghastly tooth. The second one, judging from appearances, was "Carabosse", the most deadly enemy of orthopaedie establishments. Both of them grimaced at us in horrible fashion. The first one showed her frightful tooth at my daughter, whose youth awoke her appetite. The second, crippled one shook her head and brandished a crutch as though to break my son's back, for his slim, upright figure seemed to horrify her. But the third one, who was young and good-looking, jumped lightly onto the edge of the ditch and, putting a cape round her shoulders, made a sign with her hand and set off in front of us. She was, indeed, a good little fairy, but under her highland disguise, she pleased tö call herself *Perica de Pier Bruno*.

Perica is the nicest Majorcan individual that I have met. She and my little goat are the only two living beings with whom I have left a small part of my heart in Valldemosa. The goat would have been ashamed to show itself covered in mud like the young girl; but when the latter had walked a little way through the wet grass, her bare feet became not exactly white, but certainly as beautiful as those of an Andalusian woman; and her happy smile, her trusting and inquisitive chatter, and her natural, simple politeness, convinced us we had found a veritable, perfect jewel. She was sixteen years old, had very delicate features, and her face was round and velvety like a peach. She had the regular lines and beautiful gràcefulness of a Greek statue. Her figure was as slender as a reed, and her bare arms were burnt brown. From beneath her coarse cloth shawl, her hair appeared flowing and wild like the tail of a young mare. She led us to the edge of the field and then made us cross a piece of sown ground, surrounded by trees and large boulders; and as I could not yet see the sea, I imagined that we were penetrating further into the mountain, and that the mischievous *Perica* was having a game with us.

But presently she opened a small gate that led out of the sown patch, and we saw a footpath which went round an enormous sugarloaf rock. We followed it and, as though by magic, we found ourselves above the sea, overlooking its vastness and the shore a league's distance down below our feet. The first effect of this unexpected spectacle was an attack of vertigo, and I commenced by sitting down. Gradually my head cleared and I decided to descend by the path, although it had not been designed for human feet, but for the hoofs of goats. What I saw was so beautiful that I suddenly felt I had, not seven league boots, but the wings of a swallow in my brain; and I began to go round the great limestone needles which rose like giants a hundred feet high along the steep coast-line, constantly on the lookout for a small cove that bit into the land on my right, and where some fishing boats looked as small as flies.

All at once I saw the totally blue sea all around me. The path had lost itself, I don't know where. Perica was shouting above my head, and my children, who were following me on all fours, began to shout even louder. I turned round and saw my daughter weeping copiously. I went back to find out what the matter was, and after a moment's investigation I realised there was good cause for my children's terror and distress. Another step and I would have descended far more rapidly than I wanted, for the rock on which I was venturing overhung and rose sheer from the little cove, where its base had been deeply eroded by the sea.

When I saw the danger into which I had led my children, I had a terrible fright; but after taking them to a place of safety, behind one of the gigantic sugarlcaf rocks, a fresh enthusiasm invaded me to see the bottom of the cove and the interior of the worn away cliff.

Never had I seen anything equal to what I was witnessing, and my imagination overflowed. I went down by another path, seizing hold of the underbrush, and clasping the sharp points of stones, each one of which marked a fresh descent of the path. At last I began to catch a glimpse of the immense mouth of the excavated cavern where the waves were pounding with a queer harmony. I don't know what magic chords I thought I would hear, nor what unknown world I was deceiving myself I had discovered, but my son, frightened and a little angry, came down and tried to drag me back. I came back to earth in a most unromantic manner, and sat down like a rational person; luckily I didn't fall forwards, for that would have been the end of me and my adventure. My son reproached me so forcibly for my foolhardiness that I abandoned my purpose, but not without a regret that has pursued me ever since; for my shoes become heavier every year, and I feel that the wings that I had then will never sprout again to take me to similar shores.

It is true, however, and I know it as well as anybody, that what you behold with the eye is not as good as what you see in your dreams, although this is only strictly correct in the matter of things artistic and man's handiwork. As far as I am concerned, whether because my imagination is ordinarily lazy, or because God is more talented than I am (which would not be impossible), I have often discovered nature to be more beautiful than I had surmised, and I don't remember having found it sullen and unpleasant, except when I was also in a black mood.

I will never forgive myself for not having gone right round that rock. It's possible I may have seen the sea-goddess, Amphitrite, there in person, under a vault of mother-of-pearl, with her forehead crowned by whispering sea-weed. Instead of this I was only able to admire needles of limestone rock, some rising from ravine to ravine, others descending like stalactites from cavern to cavern, and all taking on strange shapes and fantastic attitudes. The trees, of prodigious growth, bent over and half uprooted by the wind, leaned over the abyss, from the bottom of which another mountain rose up to the sky, a mountain of crystal, diamond and sapphire. The sea, viewed from a considerable height,

187

produces the illusion, as we know, of a vertical plain. Explain it if you can, but it is so.

My children insisted on taking back some plants. The most beautiful liliaceae in the world grow amongst those crags. We all three finally pulled up the bulb of a scarlet amaryllis, but it was so heavy that we couldn't carry it back to the Cartuja. My son cut a piece off this wonderful plant about the size of one's head to show to our patient. Perica, who was loaded with a bundle of sticks she had picked up on the way, and which kept brushing us in the face at every rapid twist and turn, accompanied us to the outskirts of the village. We invited her to come on to the Cartuja so that we could give her a small present, which I had great difficulty in persuading her to accept. Poor Perica! You didn't know, and you will never know, how good it was to find out that among the "monkeys" there was one gentle, charming, helpful human being, who had no mental reservations. That night we rejoiced that we should not have to leave Valldemosa without having met a sympathetic individual in that beautiful place.

CHAPTER V

B ETWEEN the two excursions I have briefly described, the first one and the last one we did in Majorca, there were several others which I will not relate, for fear of boring the reader with a tale of enthusiasm for a widespread natural beatuy, scattered with houses outrivalling each other in picturesque appeal, pretty little cottages, palaces, churches and monasteries. If any of our landscape painters decide to visit Majorca, I recommend to them the country house called the Granja de Fortuny, with the valley of citrus trees which opens out in front of its marble columns, and the road which leads up to it. But without going as far as there, it is not possible to take a few steps in this enchanted island without having to stop at every bend in the road, sometimes to look at an Arab water tank shaded by palm trees, or at a stone cross, a delicate work of the 15th century, and sometimes to pause at the edge of a grove of olive trees.

There is nothing to equal the appearance and queer shapes of the olive trees, those ancient benefactors of Majorca. The Majorcans date the most recent plantation back to the time when the island was occupied by the Romans. I will not dispute it, because I have no means of proving the contrary, even if I wanted to. When I saw the formidable look, the disproportionate bulk and the fantastic attitudes of these mysterious trees, my imagination willingly accepted them as contemporaries of Hannibal. When you stroll in the evening under their shade, it is necessary to remember that they are trees, for if you credit your eyes and imagination, you will be seized with terror in the middle of all these fantastic monsters: some bent over towards you like enormous dragons, with mouths agape and wings outspread; some coiled up on themselves like drowsy boa constrictors; others wrapped round each other like gigantic wrestlers. Here, you will find a galloping centaur, carrying some hideous monkey on his crupper; there, a nameless reptile devouring a panting deer; further on, a satyr dancing with a he-goat a little less ugly than itself; and often, a single tree, split, gnarled, twisted and deformed, which you would take for a group of ten different trees, and representing several monsters united to one single head, as horrible as an Indian fetish, and crowned by a single green branch at the apex. Anyone interested who glances at Laurens's engravings need not fear that the artist has exaggerated the appearance of the olive trees he drew. He could have chosen even more extraordinary examples; and I hope that one fine day the "Magasin pittoresque", that amusing and indefatigable popularizer of art and nature, will undertake to reproduce for us some of these first-class illustrations.

In order to get some idea of the impressive appearance of these sacred trees, from which one always expects to hear prophetic voices issuing, and of the glittering sky against which their harsh silhouettes are vigorously outlined, you would need nothing less than the bold and brilliant brush of Rousseau.[1] The limpid waters, in which the asphodels and myrtles are reflected, would on the other hand call for Dupré. Regions where the countryside is disposed in a more orderly fashion, where nature, although growing freely, seems

1.   Pierre Étienne Théodore Rousseau (1812-67), one of the greatest French landscape painters, is not well known to the public because the Salon was hostile to his work, and for many years prohibited him from exhibiting his masterpieces. (*Author's note.*)

to acquire a classical and haughty aspect through an excess of affectation, would without doubt tempt the severe Corot. But to portray the craggy, brambled ground where there are masses of various kinds of grass and wild flowers, and old tree stumps, and where weeping willows incline over hidden streams in which the stork comes and steeps its long legs, I would have liked to have had ready to hand in my pocket like a magic wand, Huet's engraving chisel.

How many times, when I looked at some old Majorcan gentleman standing on the threshold of his faded and dilapidated mansion, have I thought of Descamps, the great master of serious caricature, upgraded to the class of historical painting, the man of genius who can infuse spirit, animation, poetry, in a word, life, to the very walls. The beautiful, suntanned children who played in our cloister dressed up as monks would have delighted him. He would have had there monkeys galore, and angels at their side, pigs with human faces, and cherubs as well, mixed up with the piglets and just as dirty. But above all, he would have had Perica, as lovely as Galatea, splashed with mud like a water-spaniel, and laughing in the sun, as evertyhing does that is good on earth. But it is you, Eugène, my old friend, my dear artist, whom I would have liked to take to the mountain at night, when a livid moon was flooding the place with light.

It was in beautiful country that I was once on the point of being drowned with my poor son of fourteen, who certainly didn't lack courage as I lacked the ability to see how nature that night had become super-romantic, mad to a degree, and more than awe-inspiring. We had left Valldemosa, my son and I, to go and argue about the Pleyel piano with the ferocious customs officers in Palma. The morning had been perfectly clear and the roads passable; but when we were going through the town it began to pour with rain. We didn't worry about it, because we didn't yet know what it could mean. The rain in France doesn't last more than two hours; one cloud succeeds another, and between the two there is a respite. In Majorca a persistent cloud settles on the island, and stays there until it has completely rained itself out. This can take forty to fifty hours, or four to five days, without any stop and even without lessening in intensity.

Towards sunset we set off back in the carriage, hoping to arrive at the Cartuja in three hours. We took seven, and we nearly finished by sleeping with the frogs at the bottom of an unexpected and impromptu lake. The coachman was in a very bad temper; he had already put a thousand difficulties in our way against starting back; his horse wasn't properly shod, the mule was lame, the axle broken, and I don't know what else! We were beginning to know the Majorcans well enough not to let ourselves be deceived, and we made him get up onto his seat where he sat with a grim expression on his face. He didn't sing, he refused our cigars, and didn't shout curses at his animal, all of which was a bad sign. He was full of the direst forebodings. He was hoping to frighten us, and began by taking the worst of the seven known routes home. This led along a sunken road which sank deeper and deeper until we reached the bed of the torrent and tried to cross it. But we were soon in difficulties; the water, which was always ready to overflow, had opened a breach in the road, and we were engulfed in a roaring, raging river.

As soon as the surly coachman, who had reckoned on our being afraid, saw that we were determined to go on in spite of everything, he lost his composure and began to curse and swear enough to bring the heavens about us. The channels of hewn stone which carried the water from its source to the city, had become full to the point of bursting, like the frog in the fairy tale. Then, uncontrolled, the water had spread all over the place, forming first pools and swamps, after that lakes, and finally reaching the sea to form inlets in the land everywhere. Very soon our driver didn't know what saint to invoke, nor what devil to deliver himself up to. His feet had a sorely needed bath, for which we didn't feel in the least sorry. The small carriage was well closed, and we were still dry, but, minute by minute, as my son put it, "the tide was rising". We pushed forward at random receiving terrible shakings, and falling into potholes, with the presentiment that the last one would be our grave. Finally we lurched so

192

much that the mule stopped, as though to collect itself before giving up the ghost. The coachman got up and began to climb onto the top of the bank by the road, which at that point was at the same height as his head; but he stopped when he saw, in the twilight, that the supposed bank was nothing other than the Valldemosa water duct transformed into a river, and which, at intervals, was cascading down onto our track, also turned into a river, but a little lower down.

It was a tragi-comical moment. I felt a certain apprehension for myself, and a great fear for my son. I looked at him and saw how he was laughing at the figure cut by the coachman, who was standing astride on the shafts of the carriage; he was gauging the depth, and didn't appear to be at all amused at us. When I saw my son perfectly calm and happy, I put my trust again in God. I felt that the boy instinctively knew what his fate would be, and I surrendered to that intuition which children cannot explain, but which spreads like a cloud or a ray of sunshine over their countenances.

The coachman, when he perceived that there was no hope of abandoning us to our lot, became resigned to sharing it with us, and, suddenly turning heroic, said to us in a fatherly voice:

"Don't be afraid, my children!"

Then he let out a great shout and lashed his mule. The animal stumbled, fell, struggled up, stumbled again, and straightened up half drowned. The carriage sank to one side.

"Gee up!" yelled the driver.

The carriage lurched towards the other side.

"Gee up! Gee up! Once more!" he repeated.

Ominous creakings came from the vehicle; it gave some prodigious bounds, and emerged triumphant from its trial like a ship that has scraped the reefs without breaking up.

It seemed we were saved, and we were dry. But it was necessary to renew this sort of nautical journey in a wagonette a dozen times before reaching the mountain. But at that point the mule, at the end of its strength and frightened by the noise of the torrent and wind which came down from the heights, began to recoil towards the edge of the chasm.

We leapt out and we each manhandled one of the wheels, while the coachman pulled "Master Aliboron" by his long ears. We had to get out and do this I don't know how many times, and at the end of two hours ascent, during which we hardly covered half a league, the mule was brought to a stop on a bridge trembling in every limb; so we decided to leave the driver, the carriage and the animal there, and continue on foot to the Cartuja.

It didn't turn out to be an easy task. The steep roadway had become a boisterous torrent, which needed a good pair of legs to contend with. Other small, rapid, recently formed rivulets of water noisily descended from the lofty crags, and suddenly discharged on our right onto the track, and we had to hurry to get ahead of them, or risk crossing them for fear that they might any instant become impassable. The rain was falling in streams. Enormous clouds, blacker than ink, kept on hiding the face of the moon. And then, enveloped in the greyish, impenetrable darkness, buffeted by the impetuous wind, conscious of the tree tops swaying over our heads, and hearing the pine trees snapping and the stones rolling around us, we were forced to stop and wait until, as a witty poet once said, Jupiter blew out the candle.

In these intervals of light and shade you would have seen, my dear Eugène, the sky and the earth alternately lighting up and growing dim with the strangest and most sinister reflections and shadows. Whenever the moon recovered its splendour and seemed about to prevail in a corner of the azure sky, swiftly swept clear by the wind, some dark clouds would suddenly arrive like spectres, eager to enfold it in the folds of their shrouds. They flowed over it, and now and then tore themselves apart to show us the moon more beautiful and more compassionate than before. Then the mountain, shining with cataracts and strewn with trees uprooted by the storm, gave us an idea of the chaos. It reminded us of that magnificent Witches' Sabbath that we have seen in some dream, and which appeared to have been painted by an unknown brush, dipped into the red and blue waves of the mythical Phlegethon and Erebus. And hardly had we looked at

194

this hellish scene, which was there in reality before our eyes, than the moon, devoured by the monsters in the sky, disappeared and left us in the middle of a bluish limbo, where we seemed to float like clouds, for we couldn't even see the ground on which we were venturing our feet.

At last we reached the pass in the final mountain and we were out of all danger, once we had left the watercourses behind us. We were overwhelmed with fatigue, and we were barefoot, or nearly so. It took us three hours to cover that last league.

However the fine days returned, and the steamer "Mallorquin" was able to renew its weekly tripts to Barcelona. Our invalid didn't seem well enough to stand the crossing, but neither was he capable of puttimg up with another week in Majorca. The situation was dreadful. There were days when I lost hope and courage. To console us, Maria Antonia and her friends in the village repeatedly made for our benefit the most edifying predictions regarding our future:

"That consumptive friend of yours", they said, "will go to hell; firstly because he is tubercular, and secondly because he doesn't go to confession".

"If that happens, when he is dead we won't bury him in consecrated ground; nobody else will give him burial, so you and your friends will have to get on best you can. How you're going to overcome that problem I don't know, because I won't help."

"Nor I."

"Nor I."

At last we departed from the island, and I have already related what sort of people and hospitality we found on board the Majorcan ship.

When we arrived in Barcelona, we were so anxious to finish for ever our contact with this inhuman race, that I hadn't the patience to wait until the end of the disembarkation. I wrote a note to the Port Commandant, *Señor Belves,* and sent it to him by a launch. Almost at once he collected us in his cutter, and took us on board the "Maléagre".

195

When we set foot on this fine frigate, as spick and span as a drawing-room, and saw ourselves surrounded by kind, intelligent people, receiving the generous and solicitous enquiries of the Captain, the doctor, the officers and the whole crew, and shaking hands with the delightful and witty French Consul, M. Gautier d'Arc, we jumped for joy on the bridge and cried out from the bottom of our hearts, "Long live France!"

It seemed to us as if we had sailed round the globe, and left behind us the savages of Polynesia for the civilized world.

The moral of this narrative, maybe ingenuous but sincere, is that man was not made to live with the trees, the stones, the clear sky, the azure sea, the flowers, and the mountains but with his fellow creatures. In the tempestuous days of youth, we imagine that solitude is the great refuge against peril, and a great remedy for the wounds in the battle of life. This is a grave error, and experience of life teaches us that where we cannot live in peace with our neighbours, neither does there exist poetic admiration nor artistic delights capable of filling the gap in our hearts.

I had always dreamed of living in the desert, and every candid dreamer will confess to having had the same obsession at some time. But, believe me, my friends, we are too warm hearted to be able to do without each other, and the best thing we can do is to bear with one another mutually; for we are like children born of the same mother, who torment each other, quarrel, and even fight, but who, nevertheless, cannot part company.